Unleashed

ISBN 979-8-9865280-5-2 (Paperback Edition)

Printed and bound in the United States of America
January 2023

Author's photograph taken by:
Emari Lewis at The Dream Center, Ybor City 2022

Published by Sula Too Publishing Tampa, Florida
For information about this title or to order books and/or electronic media,
contact the publisher: Sula Too Publishing
www.sulatoo.com/publishing 813-200-8878

Unleashed
Celebrating My Dignity

By

Elizabeth P. Brooks

Poetic Muse Contents

Author's Page

Elizabeth P. Brooks
Daugther of
Trinidad & Tobago

Pioneer - Elizabeth migrated to New York City at the age of 20. She left her immediate family behind, in pursuit of the American Dream. Years later, she relocated to Los Angeles, California to raise her children. She indulged in bi-coastal living at two different periods in her life.

It was much later as an older adult Elizabeth pursued her education at CUNY, Lehman College in the Bronx. She was accepted into the Scholar's program and graduated with a degree in Sociology magna cum laude. Upon graduation she was hired by New York Public Library and immediately enrolled at Pratt Institute, Brooklyn to obtain a MS (LIS). Her greatest joy was serving the community, and empowering the public by providing them with access to information. Her first job in the NYPL was at George Bruce branch in Harlem where the patron/user/customer showed much gratitude.

In 2000, she returned to Los Angeles and accepted the challenge to manage a branch of the Pasadena Public Library, in an economically depressed neighborhood. Elizabeth built a team who recognized the value of their work and as a result they brought hope, pride and structure to their community. Each member of the team received a Certificate of Special Congressional Recognition from the office of Congressman Adam Schiff in recognition of invaluable service to the community. She participated in a Quality of Life Session in the City of Pasadena and presented on The Power of One: how YOU can make a difference.

Elizabeth now calls Tampa (Champa) Bay home. She is energetic, outgoing, loves people, the sound of laughter and is deeply concerned about humanity, lifelong learning and the need for social justice.

By profession she is a reference librarian. She volunteers as an adult literacy tutor and is a member of Grace Family Church, Ybor City FL. She is a performance poet and has had several poems and non-fiction essays published in Indiana Voice Journal an online publication in addition to a self-published chapbook, You May Applaud Now and other poems. She has written a column A Call to Love on Spirit Fire Review an online publication and she is also a contributor to Huffington Post.

She has received acclaim as a Contemporary Black Poet
https://slulibrary.saintleo.edu/c.php?g=1057126&p=7682252

This book is retrieved from pop up memories indelibly carved into my mind, spirit and soul. It defines where I was, who I am, and where I am going. Some of my work is taken from my journals, scrap paper, and a previously published chapbook "You May Applaud Now and Other poems" a Boldly Into Grace BIG publication and some published essays. I am still connecting the dots and forever celebrating HUMAN DIGNI-TY. This is my Why! I write to speak to the wail of pain that I hear, loud and clear but it is ignored by some and disregarded. I hear the sound, the rumble, the inner turmoil. In the silence, I hum to the pain and in the dead of night, I rock my body to sleep for oppressed and bewildered people. I listen and I speak to the pain of inequality and injustice, and I obey and I write, too early in the morning or after a numbed night. Yes, love wins every time I speak to my pain.

Some words bring ill will; others bring deceit, condemnation, and defeat. But my words are not empty they are full of gifts. My words want to thank you, to love you and to empower you. There is sacrifice, truth, comfort, more importantly, healing, gratitude and conviction in my words.

To my posse who offered their encouragement for me to continue to write despite physical pain and medical issues. Your support and love in the knowledge that I needed healing. I had to step up and step into God's plan of serving others. Spiritually, I am healed, and I need to walk in the manifestation of that healing, daily. We know hurt people hurt people and we know the converse is true. I am one of the healed people who will heal people. This is a demonstration that no matter what is going on, how low the valley, how high the mountain, or how brutal the storm with lightning, strong winds, and thunder, I must focus on my spirit and my gift and do what is required of me.

It's more than three years ago since I was supposed to have back surgery to regain 30% mobility. I believe I have regained almost 90% mobility without surgery, Thank You Jesus! Alleluia! That debilitating condition was almost unbearable. I was in the wilderness for four years. I surrendered totally to our Holy Father and was showered with His blessings, grace, and mercy. During that time of fear and lack, I experienced the purpose of affliction and what was available to me, the Power of the Holy Spirit. There were times I could not process a thought to speak intelligibly or answer a question. I would meditate for several days when someone asked me a question and I could not answer because I was still processing the information. At times, I could not recognize my monitor to keep a log of my medical daily statistics. On one occasion, an unrecognized voice spoke through my lips when I was trying to speak to a friend, BT. She had called me on the phone, out of concern. I kept telling her I could not talk. I was struggling to formulate words. My words were unintelligible, confused, my thoughts without focus, incoherent. I did not go through a difficult time the last three and a half years, but I actually grew through that difficult time and received my healing, which LORD have Mercy, I know is ongoing. I am showered with unbelievable blessings, grace, divine favor, and mercy.

Dedication:

To my beautiful and generous family, full of abundant love,
joy, and laughter
The large and accommodating "Marcano Race"
&
The Brooks'
It could not have been done without
the Excelsior "Ever Upward" Vibe and
the rich heritage of Fyzabad.
To my colleagues who encourage me to write
CAM and JD, CT.
Most of all, I extend deep gratitude for the precious Angel that
my Holy Father sent to minister unto me. He practically never
left my side. He catered to me beyond anyone's expectation, full
of humility and dedication. He filled my every need required to
promote my healing and to regain trust in humanity.
Thank U AJ!
Hooray! My gratitude is thrust out to my awesome and talented
publisher, Sula Too Publishing for support and encouragement.

Come and See

What the LORD has done

Come

In The Beginning

Journal entry   **4/29/2015**

For 10 days I lusted, coveted sleep. The writing was flowing out of me. In the middle of the night, I was awakened and compelled to write. I had written several poems by then. I remember telling my mentor Barbara G the day before my chapbook launch that the writing is not leaving me and she said, "that's how gifts flow". But I was immature in my spirit and I did not get it that my writing is a gift from God. We both laughed when I responded, "but I don't want to be like Michael Jackson." If I recall correctly one of his big complaints was, he could not stop the music in his head, so he could sleep.

On about the 11th or the 12th night, I slept like a baby for 2 nights. I awakened the next morning in bed surrounded by my journals, tablet, Bible and a newly written poem. I woke up in a fog, a distant place. None of it appeared familiar to me. I was detached from it. I actually said, "where did this come from?" I could not own it.

My writing was a foreign thing. I decided to read my Bible, a brand new experience for me. In the fourth book of Numbers, Chapters 11:17, I read about these wretched ungrateful people in the wilderness and how they complained and blasphemed against God. I recognized that I was one of them. How could I be so ungrateful, unfaithful to a faithful God who is my life-giver, my provider, and my protector?

I fell on my face like Aaron and Moses and pleaded with God, that I have sinned ignorantly. I begged HIM for forgiveness. I realized He was showing me who He was - I heard it once said, you truly don't negotiate a gift, you receive it.

I have always asked God to show up in my life; show me what my talent is. Use me for something extraordinary because there is so much work for me to do to further His kingdom. I've pledged my faithfulness to HIM. I have been tested and proven in my spiritual maturity. He allowed me to discern that. I now stay in close proximity to HIM to hear His voice. I wake up with a smile on my face anytime I hear the whisper of the Holy Spirit, and I write. I promised HIM I would write for 24 hours if He wants me to do so. Thy will be done Holy Father.

Last week after leaving "Beautiful" our women's group at Grace Family Church, I said to HIM, "It looks like tonight would be a long night." But He let me ruminate.

"Stand in awe and sin not: commune with your own heart upon your bed and be still. Selah". Psalm 4:4.

My intention is to wait and to act on HIS every whim.

During my adult life attending church was not a practice of mine. I did not raise my children in the church. (As a matter of fact, we did "The Transformation of Man", the EST training by Werner Erhard) a powerful discipline which brings aware-ness of Making a Difference, Living with Integrity and cre-ating meaningful relationships, The Hunger Project etc., But when we visited my Mom, I would accompany the family and we had a deep spiritual connection. I reminisced because I was raised in the church, the Catholic Church and even wanted to become a nun and when my son was born, I wanted him to become a priest. My oldest sister asked in disbelief, "Are you Italian? My cynical husband said, "She has so many sins she wants to sacrifice the baby to pray for her." During an early session of Beautiful, our women's group, I announced to the group that I was going to be baptized that weekend. It was at that time that my poetry writing had begun to flow. The first poem that I wrote during the sessions was titled "Beautiful" celebrating the love, grace, power, goodness, and the majesty of women. And in the blink of an eye without intent or knowledge, I was composing a chapbook for publication. I had discovered I was walking in the Light.

I John 1 :5 This is the message that we have heard from Him and declare to you. God is Light and in Him there is no darkness at all.

I John 1:7 But If we walk in the Light as He is in the Light, we have fellowship with one another and the blood of Jesus the son purifies us. (NIV)

As we wrapped up the first semester of Beautiful, I was asked to give my testimony. Testimony?? Do I have a testimony? What does testimony mean to me? To testify...hmm! My testimony was revealed to me.

My testimony: Moses had his anointed rod, Aaron his budding rod which blossomed into almonds. David had his slingshot. And I have to accept the fact that I have my anointed pen. "And be not conformed to the world; but be transformed by the renewing of your mind, that ye may prove what is that good and acceptable, and the perfect will of God."
(Romans 12-2 KJV). "But the manifestation of the Spirit is given to everyman to profit withal" (I Corinthians Chapter 12:7) .

The entire chapter should be compulsory reading. It covers spiritual gifts for different uses. My turning point: I showed faith in God's provision.

Journal entry   **6/14/2015**

> *I am available and receptive.*
>
> *I have experienced and embraced*
> *Something more, the Holy Spirit,*
> *More of his Glory, more of His Presence*
> *More of His Grace, more of His Love*
> *And more of His Honor and Mercy.*
>
> *He does not define me*
> *His love refines me*
> *I am one of His precious gifts,*
> *I am filled with seeds of greatness.*

Yet, with all that growth and declaration, I reverted to my old habits. Many nights I pleaded and covered my head with my pillow "Oh please not now Holy Spirit." 2020.
I really could not find a comfortable place to sit since my back ailment.

Elizabeth P Brooks

Morning, Noon and Ignite

Arise, shine, for your light has come and the glory of the LORD
has risen upon you. For behold darkness shall cover the earth,
and thick darkness the peoples; but the Lord will arise upon
you, and His glory shall be seen by you. Isaiah 60:1-2 ESV

Some days interruptions and joy could be thwarted by events
and circumstance. The challenge then for me, is to recognize
inaction, disobedience, and hesitance. I reflect and renew my
mind knowing who I am. I recommit readily to not grieve the
Holy Spirit, my guide. The day could possibly be in full bloom
by the time of that revelation. Paths are crossed. I missed op-
portunities to shed His light.

Years ago, one of my managers in the workplace asked me
about my professional goals and my answer to her was "I am
on assignment." I was actually scratching my head when I re-
sponded. I had no idea what that meant and why I said it.
That conversation did not continue any further. Much later,
I understood in my spirit, what being on assignment meant.
And I embrace that knowledge with a responsibility to share
God's love; my experience of my faith; my spiritual growth and
the love and ultimate sacrifice of our Lord Jesus Christ. Some
people do not understand my energy. In my most recent past I
would try to tone my energy down. I learned so many of life's
lessons for such a time as this. I realize we all have different gifts
and are on different assignments. I have work to do, and no one
can take my joy away. We all bring different gifts to the table. I
ask God to lead me to the people he wants to rise up today. It
is not about me, Lord!

As a child, many times my father told me "You walk with alac-
rity," and I did not know what he meant. One day I asked, and
he explained, "Like you have something important to do and
somewhere to go." That little girl full of passion was in train-
ing, looking for a purpose, knowing there was something more.

I have always talked to strangers, and I found a way to make others listen face-to-face to what I have to say now; even if it is an audience of one, in the street, park or parking lot. I am always escorting people from one point to the other.

I share my poetry that is inspired by the Lord, and I share my story. I ask professors to allow me to share my poetry in their Sociology and Psychology classes. My passion and my ability to memorize my work surprises everyone. They usually ask, "How is that possible?" With boldness, I declare it is a gift from God. I inform them, that in daily prayer I ask God to grant me excellent memory recall, short term, and long term because I have a lot of work to do for His glory. (My mother had Alzheimer's).

Throughout my entire life it has been difficult for me to ask for anything. I was the contented child. Now I ask boldly, and I receive. Students have invited me to perform at their sorority functions and others at cultural events, and women's ministries; My greatest joy was spending the day and performing poetry for a middle school in Temple Terrace. I also performed at the final presidential debate watch party, (and prior visit) at Hillary Clinton's camp. I keep planting seeds that I know you my friends will water and vice versa.

The first poem I remember writing as a child was "A Song for Jesus." Throughout my day I smile to myself, and I ask my Holy Father, "Father why do you love me so much?" And I pray to Him, giving thanks for my talents, gifts, and character-istics and for protecting me, His delinquent know-it-all child. I thank Him for Jesus. Oh, what a love affair! My spirit is in constant joy. Throughout the day I acknowledge Him and con-fess my love to Him. "Thy word is a lamp unto my feet, and a light unto my path." Psalm 119:105(KJV) I acknowledge His constant presence in my life as my provider and my protector. Even with fear I am compelled to pray, Father send me, there is so much work to be done for Your glory.

A gleam of light with passion and purpose has erupted whether sun, rain, or storm. I see You, Lord! I hear your call. You are calling us, Lord. It is inconceivable the depths you go to, to stir our spirit, our souls; to capture our imagination and our emotions. Your promise is in the sweet fragrance of a flower, all of nature; a pinch of pungent rotting ripe fruit that has been tossed. You are beautiful, loving and are everywhere. I see you in the beauty and joy of text on paper and in the sweat on the brow of a brother or sister. I see the innocence and hope of our children in school yards or leaving school with school bags. I see your reflection in the strength and dignity of people without homes – including our veterans. I look them in the eye and acknowledge them. Lord, Your children are not invisible. I am very clear whether I experience trauma or create my drama, my job in life is to engage Your children with a smile, a nod, a knowing look. No matter where I am, I offer common decency, love, and courtesy. I give a hand, share, and say a kind word. Interestingly enough, today I heard a politician say. "If everything you think about is, what is in it for me? Then you are a loser." Father God, in the middle of all of our resentments, disappointments and observations You give us an opportunity daily to experience Your magnificence and the power of Your love.

Then dusk comes and You ignite the sky for all of us, oppressors and the oppressed, moaning and groaning in many voices, and different languages. It is like having candles on a birthday cake or fireworks and piñatas from heaven, bursting with love, joy, and gladness, for all of us. I inhale deeply and get that fully charged aroma of Your sweet fragrance and a Holy kiss. With gratitude, I consume the breath of life again and again, infinite. I look and listen, always attuned to moods around and modes as You design my encounters. Oh, Holy Father, send me!

You are my breath
You are my spirit
You are my soul![1]

Journal entry   **2017**

No one understands the depth of my pain, the strain to climb steps, to bend over to pick up something or to put on a shoe, slip-on, lace up or Velcro.

---

1 © Elizabeth P. Brooks Published in Spiritfirereview.com (column A Call to Love)

Elizabeth P Brooks

Who Knew

Who knew
It would be a challenge
to make my bed, tuck a sheet.
My laundry bag stayed
packed for weeks
unable to take it
downstairs
afraid I would have
to bring it back up
after being washed.

Who knew
I would have to
boil drinking water
because it is too painful
to go to the store
tearfully, I stood online
at CVS with a gallon
too heavy in hand.

Who knew
I would be wearing two braces
one for my upper back
and one for my waist
Who knew
I would have to
go to bed with an icepack.

Who knew
when I awake
the first thing I would
do is to put on my waist brace
so I can make my bed by noon.

Who knew
I would cry in public
in the parking lot
waiting helplessly
for security to carry
me back to my building
on a golf cart.

Who knew
for Easter I would
eat tofu and squash
I was afraid
to let anyone know
I was in pain and alone
I had many invitations
but pretended
I had already accepted.

Who knew
 I would
find so much solace
With God, Jesus, and my Holy Spirit.

Who knew!

Who knew I would give away all my designer
handbags and purses, satchels, pocketbooks,
because they are too heavy to carry
I could possibly carry them empty
but what is the point.

I kept one of each
a school bag sack
and a satchel.

Elizabeth P Brooks

Euphoric
The old lady wondered! Would I die of thirst, twist my wrist,
break my fingers before I unscrew the cap on this bottle to taste
the bliss of cool water?

She anticipated the gulp of the swallow and experience of the
trickle down her slender throat. Now an expression of grati-
tude of AHH! And OHM!

Here comes the blessing the trickle of drinking water
She is washed in grace. Her thirst is finally quenched.

Yesterday, a Good Day
Today, don't know
How long I have been at it
Longer than twenty minutes.

Handwashing at the kitchen sink
Unable to carry a
Heavy load to laundry
Drop off to Andy & Company
When I can stand that erect,
I wash
I rinse,
I wring
I stop before my back
yells with threats
to crack.

How my life has changed
Too many ask
What plans do you have
for the weekend?

Or very pleasantly
How was your weekend?

Even my chiropractor and
primary care doctor,
knowing the depth of my pain,
engage in small talk.

It is a social custom
asking without thinking
inappropriate violation of the norm.

However, for Christmas
my orthopedist stopped me
after our visit and walked back in and asked
Do you have relatives and friends nearby?
I said "Yes," I lied
He asked where and knowing I lied,
with emphasis he prescribed
"Do not be alone."

Groin to Saddle

There is no pain in my groin,
but it is alive and ripe with sensation.
I am on the brink of having orgasms continually
I have determined it is PGAD
Persistent genital arousal disorder!

Activity from the Pudendal nerve
No doctor could or would discuss this with me.
Male and female doctors are ignorant
Their attention is on erectile dysfunction that's
important.

I don't know how to sit or stand.
I pray and I cry,
 Should I cross my legs and squeeze my thighs
or just play dead.

Unable to blink away my tears,
I pray and I cry and I wipe my eyes
Then I pray and I cry again.

During the course of 5 months
the experience was practically 24-7 of agony,
sheer horror and hell
with very intermittent relief.

When I mentioned my predicament with urgency
my doctors looked at me incredulously
They were devoid of comfort or comment, speechless.

Maybe my neurologist was awaiting
the results from my MRI
It's a mystery why my MRI follow up visit was
cancelled.

At any given time in the wee hours or high noon;
I deliberated going to the emergency room
There is no basis for this sensory response,

After doing research
I finally had the courage to tell my chiropractor,
who was treating me
for the fall that almost ruined my life.

When I mentioned to him
consistent and unwanted orgasms
he almost smiled
I told him it's not funny and
I know you could fix it.

At the end of one of my 3 times a week,
life-saving sessions
As I returned to my car,
I realized the orgasms had diminished
Further research informed me, my chiropractor
had manipulated my pelvic floor
That was a blessing with reduced intensity,
thankfully though temporarily.

I cannot contain the tears that's
streaming down my face
It's three o'clock I have been up
three hours since my pee break
Maybe I should try to sleep supine
with my knees flexed and thighs spread.

Relief really comes when the
spasms in my groin
retreat to my saddle even then, it reminds me,
it is there to haunt me.

Elizabeth P Brooks

2020

I am unable to remove washed clothing
from my washing machine
or clean my refrigerator without a claw grabber
while sitting on a walker. Yes I'm now using a walker

My upsweep hairstyle in a bun is evidence,
a testament to my progress
I was unable to lift my hands above my shoulder.

Many close accidents
of pulling down a hot pot while cooking,
if I turned around because of dizzy spells.

I could have only functioned
within 10-minute increments
then back to bed.
Some nights I returned to my bedroom
after a bathroom break 2 or 3 in the morning
And I actually thought I had just returned home.

During the first few weeks of COVID lock-down, I was hospitalized for excessive high blood pressure and not one of my PCP doctors or nurse, or pharmacist in or out of the hospital, or my insurance provider determined there were contraindications with medications. Prayer works and God my provider blessed me with the answer. "Do your own research." I did research! It took me another year for more improved recovery due to trials and more trials of other medications from the doctors, I did not need. A test of my blood sugar revealed my blood sugar was high. "I said that was my COVID sin. I was eating chocolate." I was given a prescription I should not had taken. I stopped eating chocolate immediately and have not had any since. The next test revealed my blood sugar was under control.

Having cause for deep concern, I had to become very insistent. My doctor finally agreed with me when in a rage, I was asked "What do you want me to do? And I revealed what drugs I should be on. The doctor complied and noticed my health improved and added," you are right by the end of the year all will be well." More healing, Thank you, Holy Father! I continue to remind everyone who knew of my condition to always question doctors and check medications, particularly in the elderly when there is no improvement, memory loss, or and patient health declines. My doctors never considered my lifestyle. The methodology used was one size fits all. Within the last two years I lost over 16 pounds and my doctors appeared concerned. At every weigh in I was told "Do not lose any more weight."

Elizabeth P Brooks

The Church Has Failed Us
(Not My Church)

Twisted Christians self-absorbed pedaling sin
still obsessed with the color of my skin
ignoring Jesus, humility and Christiandom
they have become their own God
living like Pharaohs, Pharisees and Sadducees
not accepting the challenge of the day
which will make them too uncomfortable

Instead of spreading truth and joy
they are selective in their choice of verse
mouth filled with gravel.

They can watch me in the eye and talk about tithe.
I have to pray and say," Father, forgive them
for they know not what they do" and
every Sunday my faith and trust
in the word of Jesus kept me hoping and
waiting on them to address their stain of sin
on all their universal platforms.

While I watch them sidestep a hustle and flow.
And I confess repeatedly
I am on the edge of my seat in full view of the
ugliness.

Seats are full no question or challenge
about who made their pew-.

The issue of who built your pew should be
of paramount concern the same as it were
with Jesus and the moneychangers in the temple
that form of slavery is more profit in their pockets.

They are not counting Black Lives,

not counting any Indigenous People lives
or any people of color.

How many lives have you destroyed for centuries,
with Post Traumatic Slave Syndrome?

How many children have you fathered?

How many children have you dragged
from their mothers' breast to put up on your auction
block?

How many men have you dragged from their family
out of greed to earn a dollar with no turning back?

Yet you talk about fatherless children.
You are the architect!
Your actions are depraved like a savage.

Journal entry   **2020**

And Jesus Wept
Borders, bridges, cages, tunnels, tension, transition, immigration I can't hear you! Jesus said what you do to the least of them you have done to me.
All of these children belong to God, yet you are so glaringly hypocritical in tone and choices where are your voices?

I'm trying to gain insight to feel your compassion or conviction, but you are side stepping with blatant tunneled vision more dangerous than the tunnels which young children have to migrate through looking for freedom.

You are dressed to kill like a socialite on television. You belong to a country club, oh you matadors. Strutting like Chauvin. Hand in the pocket, for added swagger and to inflict added pressure

Your hypocrisy is not veiled to me - I can't hear you! I can't watch you anymore. Your demeanor shouts without a doubt You have no empathy for the killing of the Indigenous People, Black and Brown people in America- and elsewhere. I can't hear you! You are not deceiving Jesus. Jesus is weeping looking at your lack of humility and empty arrogance. You walk in the Spirit of Convenience you step into boldness with unequivocal babble.

Mocking God while Satan is leading you! Crawling up your frock. You don't recognize your voice above your noise. Jesus is still knocking at the church door. You won't let HIM come in. What happened to the Golden Rule - love your neighbor as yourself-in Genesis, Exodus, Isaiah, and Book of Ruth Sojourners are everywhere in the Bible beginning with Abraham.

Jesus is the LIGHT of the World and He also was a refugee and a revolutionary.

OH you can't resist a police officer you got to take it up after? That logic does not hold water for people of color there is no after but the hereafter. People of color are dying in custody that's a great part of the fight when adrenaline kicks in its fight or flight even being submissive one can die in custody that's the result, there is only one outcome.

Oh, help me Sweet Jesus-Save ME - I come to Thee.

2021

Scripture tells us that we have everything we need in our home. Everything has already been given to us. So I listened, obeyed and looked around my home and like the woman who had owed so many creditors in 2 Kings 4.

She discovered all that she had was a small jar of olive oil, that she poured and poured I decided to read some of my journals where I had poured my heart out as my ink spilled out.

My middle name has always been unusual to me. I was intrigued the first time I heard it. I adopted it. It means "open door" due to the resurrection. Sacred fire it represents Christ. Here I am stepping into another open door. I am on my journey, with purpose, full of passion, growing and going through this process.

I will not grieve the Holy Spirit, my comforter, counselor and my guide.

Elizabeth P Brooks

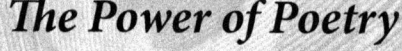

The Power of Poetry

BOOMM!

Poetry invigorates me, yet it can deplete my energy simultaneously when it tugs at my gut and stills the beat of my heart. Poetry compels me to listen to the voice of my soul. Poetry is in awe of you. Poetry loves you. Poetry will stand up and speak up and will fight for you.

The tension is to engage us to think anew. As we reflect on injustice our cries chaos and crises of our personal history

It was a little bittersweet when I helped to stir a poisoned pot which was boiling hot.

The isms bubbled up when I dared to express my soulful cry, my call to love, our heritage at an open event.

We rocked the country club with poetry and graphic video content which mirrored the truth that echoes in our souls but our presentation was not Hallmark enough. It was too Mahogany. It provoked their spirit.

It gave some cause to challenge our Freedom, Silence our Voices about Celebrating Our Humanity Our Black Experience
Yet, we spent hard earned dollars chii ching ching in 2018, Bay Scape Bistro, Plantation Drive, in Wesley Chapel. C'est la vie! But I'm discovering the power of poetry and I care enough to tell the truth and I want to change our world and celebrate humanity.

Say What!

An editor at the university claimed she loved one of my submissions.

And wanted to publish it- She said it is so timely and must be heard. If only you would make a few edits. They would publish the first stanza. She said the second stanza is just a rant. She wanted my poem dismantled to make it more palatable to her conscience. I recognize a bear trap as a challenge not defeat. So I agreed wholeheartedly. Don't mess with me! Now I have confirmation- they want to erase any recognition, hint, stain or guilt of their contamination.

But I speak BOLDLY, as I step into HIS throne of Grace. The truth cannot disappear. I must tell it like it is. My words may sometimes scar, scorch or sting; but it is a Call to love.

We are Black coals of fire burning brightly. We are Freedom Fighters, instruments of humanity. This is our heritage and my Black woman privilege.

This is My Fight!

With poetry my lips become my fist and I stake our claim BOOM!

We are the chosen ones.

BOOMM!!

Trini Spoil Chile

Trini Spoil Chile
learned everything in the home
'bout being lovin', respectful, and givin'
being a chile of Jesus, full of goodness,
joy and happiness.

That's the being taught and known -
clean body, clean clothes, clean home.
But doin' things like makin' bake, cakes
and pies - unknown. Sewin', knittin',
ironin', and cookin' passed me by.
My father said I was too small a chile.
But I did the storytellin', the dancin',
and the laughin'.

Sometimes we don't realize where
our gifts lie. I went to the movies every week.
My family sat and listened to me
regurgitate the movie I had seen line by
line, frame by frame.

When my sisters are asked did they
see a particular movie which is very vivid
in their memory, they could not remember
whether they saw it or I told it.

In the Canal

Stifling, squeezed, sunken, not wet
Surrounded by soft mounds of warmth on both sides
Even when it seemed like I could not breathe
I would push something, something soft, something
Muscular or something fat,
I could wiggle and squiggle; remind them that I am
here.

I remember my father rearranging the bed
Putting it next to the wall so I could not fall
But I would not sleep there.
I did not want the corner
I wanted the canal, to be in the gap
that narrow dip where I could nestle, yes,
Cuddle in gap on the mattress between them
Every night they remembered how much I loved them
back.

I was there.

In the latter years there was much more struggle
to get me out of their bed
But it was evident someone had planted an echo in
my head "age of reason".

With opposition coming from my paternal
grandmother
who lived with us.

Some mornings I would wake up elsewhere
I realized I was moved during the night.
At breakfast I would pout, mad at them.

With constant talk of preparation
And instruction of catechism I

was finally weaned.

*To receive the sacrament of Holy Communion
with the Lord. An expectation, now I had reached
the age of reason.*

*But I had the luxury of sleeping in the canal with
both of them, my parents, until I was almost seven.*

*I was the baby for seven years
I don't know what that means except
I am seven years older than my baby sister.*

*Two-year-old Elizabeth Pascalle Brooks
1949 - Outside home*

They called me Elita, the diminutive form of Isabelita for Elizabeth. My daddy was taking my picture and I wanted to cry. I was scared. His camera was a big box. Then he covered his face with a black cloth and I could not see him. I was 2 years old. Someone gave me the dinner gong to hold onto to distract me. I always wondered why my teddy bear looked so strange. When I arrived in NY I realized it was a Winnie the Pooh.

Brooks Family Tree Branch

My father was born at Tragarette Road, Port of Spain. He was one of four children. Two of his younger siblings were born in Brazil. My father lived in Sao Paulo until he was seventeen. My uncle had a family in Sao Paulo, and he made very rare visits to Trinidad but wrote letters and sent many greeting cards. I remember discovering the similarity with Portuguese and Spanish. I was studying Spanish in school at that time, and I enjoyed translating his greeting cards. My eldest sister visited Sao Paulo once and met our cousins.

The only grand-parent I knew was my paternal grandmother, Maude Matilda Brooks, formerly Brown. We called her Mother. She lived with us after she returned to Trinidad from Harlem, NY where she worked as a seamstress. Mother had a beautiful steamer trunk. My Mom said "the trunk" was filled with accoutrements." The word "accoutrements" was one of my mother's favorite words, I thought. Many people in the neighborhood experienced great delight when Mother opened her trunk filled with hats, bags, clothing, and dinner gong, etc., Mother made us walk with books on our heads to teach us how to stand erect, with our shoulders back, and to walk like a young lady by putting one foot in front of the other.

My Dad was very strict yet loving. He was always teaching or introducing us to something new but not always in an inspiring way. The first time I was introduced to Socrates I was reminded of my father. He was a thinker and an achiever. We thought he was augmentative. Here is an inside family joke. We overheard Mommy when she asked Daddy "Bob why, do you want to educate me so much? I remember Mommy in those discussions attempting to change the subject… But Daddy was in his glee. My parents appeared to have two different dispositions. And as much as I loved my Daddy, sometimes his conversations were too intense. I wondered for Mommy's sake what would it be like for her if he worked on a ship and she would always be happy when he came home. He was gainfully employed by Apex Oilfield Company and he worked as a fireman with a boiler. Yet, he was the proprietor of Excelsior Printery. Excelsior means "Higher", "Onward and Upward". Go Marley! I remember Daddy taught me to dance as I stepped on his shoes. Our feet had become one and we moved to the rhythm. He liked ballroom dancing. He would kiss me purposely before he shaved, and I did not like that- the hair on his face was too rough and he would laugh.

Robert Malcolm Brooks

Gerardina Brooks

My beloved parents
Photo taken after the birth of their first child in 1939

My mother was born in Diego Martin to Paul and Paulina Edwards, formerly Marcano. The family had a rich Catholic heritage. My grandmother, called Mama, washed and ironed the altar cloths for the Catholic church in their Parrish. Diego Martin, where my mother lived, was a rich and fertile land. There was an abundance of food, ground provision like cassava, dasheen and eddo, chataigne and breadfruit. Sacks of sugar, flour and rice were purchased to add to the abundance of wild meat, like rabbits. French planters settled in Diego Martin with their slaves.

My mother's ancestors were Amerindian from Venezuela. My mother's ancestors were neither Spanish nor Indian but distinctive. Tribe unknown: such is the legacy of slavery. The family would laugh and say they were the Marcano race. In the 1800's four Marcano brothers came from Venezuela to Trinidad. They went separate ways when they arrived and were never seen again. They came from a pocket in Venezuela where French was spoken. My mother and her sisters and brothers spoke Creole and another secret language or dialect. They would interject words into their conversations, amidst sweet laughter. As children, we would leave the room then, assuming that we were not supposed to listen. My mother's lineage was practically all female. They were very enterprising and passionate, full of joy, laughter, and compassion.

I was always in awe about a story my mother frequently told about Mama. In such a patriarchal society, my mother recalled that she and her twin sister accompanied Mama from house to house to sell chocolate for a penny. Mama went through the process and made chocolate from cocoa pods. There were several cacao trees at the back of the house. That's how Mama bought the house which is still standing today and has continually been renovated. My mother's father, Paul worked at the Lighthouse in North Post and his nickname was Cockle. There is a popular story told about Cockle. A sailor had given him an item to keep in his pocket for good luck. He was supposed to carry it wherever he went. At the end of the month, Cockle went to pay the shop keepers and was told by every shop owner that he had already paid his bill, which was untrue. No one would take money from him. Cockle threw the item away into the sea.

Quite often my mother's family mentioned … "the African man was from the Yoruba tribe." He was never called by any name. It has been confirmed that we are Yoruba from Benin. An interesting part of our history is, there is an African cemetery in Diego Martin and my relatives in Trinidad have to give permission for anyone's burial there to this day. The African legacy continues.

My mother was 1 of 12 children. She and her identical twin sister were the last children. They were called Tim and Titim. My mom was Titim. Mama died when my mother was a pre-teen or early teen.

Robert & Gerardina Brooks Upbeat Dad & Mom at home in the Bronx - our weekend with my cousin FB hidden in the back with a big grin (circa 1974)

Elizabeth P Brooks

Pillar To Post

By God's Grace, Tim and Titim were not separated when Mama died but they moved around from time to time to different relatives' houses in search of a conducive home. These powerless girls went from pillar to post to avoid being molested. Then these innocent girls mastered an intangible game they called "Pillar to Post" in which they engaged with subtlety and silence to avert conflict i.e. being captured and fondled by predators; older cousins and whoever felt it was their privilege. There was always a predator in the household or neighborhood seeking another conquest. It was prevalent and unspoken. Sexual deviance and silence was part of the culture. People are generally fascinated by identical twins. They could be a distraction and sometimes an obsession. Predators primed their pumps in anticipation of a trigger squeeze as these children were bullseye in the perverse men's line of fire. Too many men were ready to seduce and comfort these children. But these girls rose to the occasion. They became closer than they ever were. They became "Siamese." They were never alone. They developed wit, resilience, and loyalty as they persevered among predators. Mommy had so much courage, though she thought she had none. She always said when you pray to God always ask Him to "Give you courage."

As an adult, my aunt returned to the family's house to raise her family. As children we spent vacation time with my Mom at the home. There were several funny moments of trying to figure out who was whose Mommy. During our visits, we would sleep camp style. Snuggle up wherever we could lay our heads. We had fun until we dropped. I distinctly remember my Mom and my aunt smelled the same, especially their armpits. It was the same special scent to me, very fragrant. There was so much comfort there probably because they nursed each other's babies.

There was a valance over one of the doorways and my aunt

would brush it with the top of her head when she passed by, and my Mom would float under the valance. One day my cousin told me "Go, that's your Mommy." She was a little embarrassed that she had snuggled up with the wrong Mommy and played with the wrong breast the previous night. She became aware when holding on to the breast she asked for some water and her Mom responded " Come Doux Doux" from another bed.

Elizabeth P Brooks

A Celebration of "The Girls"

Representative of woman, lover, wife
more importantly mother
a giver – blessed with power.

Newborns shudder at the sight,
the touch, the scent
the taste of "The Girls"
with innate wisdom, a natural aptitude
for survival to sustain life.

Babies first grasp, a teat, a tit to wit.[2]

In celebration of my Mom and my aunt who nurtured us with abundant love. Their birthday is Oct, 16.

The Call of the Child

*One of the most irresistible sounds
is the voice of a child calling for a mother.
This divine sound trumpets a blessing.*

*Every time I hear the call or cry of a child,
it is like a heartfelt prayer from the voices of my
children.
The call or cry is the prayer of a child.*

*It is sacred, a language unto itself, without accent or
nationality, infused with knowing and expectancy.
The call is an explosion of hope, trust, and love.*

*Naturally, mothers want to be there to comfort,
to listen, to love, to protect and to share.*

*At birth, when the umbilical cord is severed from
mother and child,
there is another dynamic. In that fragment of time, an
invisible cord is permanently tethered to woman and
child,
in response to the baby's cry and can be discerned.*

*We have the capacity to respond to the magnetism
that rhythm, the call of the child. The sound of the
call elicits a stimulus response like a subtle electric
charge that produces a wondrous effect.
A phenomenon!*

*I hear the echo, feel the surge, the wave - the
connectedness of women to children. It runs through
every muscle, every sinew, every drop of blood, every
tissue.*

It goes beyond biological and physiological; it is supernatural. It massages my need to spread a wing, hug to my breast, bow to see, maybe drop to a knee. We are blessed with maternal gifts. Maternal gifts in synergy, a big responsibility that is mutually advantageous.

At the call, instinctively I turn my head at the mall, street, park, or supermarket. I discover that it is not my child, but with my gaze, I ensure that child is safe. With compassion and empathy, I smile and I bless the child I look upon, regardless of creed, race, color, or nationality. I know that every blessing I give to each and every child, God multiplies those blessings I send as gifts back to my children.

This is an invitation! You are invited to the Call of the Child, hear the call, heed the cry, even the giggle, the smile, the sound of laughter and bless that child.

Smile! Let us bless everyone's sons and daughters. Stay attuned. Tap into it! Do it spontaneously! Bless the child, intentionally.

Blessings don't ask who, what, where, when or why. Those blessings are returned to us by God as abundant rewards. It's our responsibility to humanity!

Give one blessing to change our culture. One blessing to change our world![3]

My cousins' beloved paternal grandmother also lived with them. She was responsible for cooking meals.

---

3 Elizabeth P. Brooks © Copyright 2015 a version published in Spirit Fire Review

Between Sleep and Wake

Sapodilla, Mamie Sapote
Breadfruit or zaboca
Ma Petra could tell
how many and from which tree they fell

Between sleep and wake
She was in her very own food store
She mentally crossed off items needed
On her non-existent shopping list
Between sleep and wake

She calculated meals for the day
Stirred pots and pans
To feed her family
Daughter-in-law, grandchildren
And always another

There was always something to eat
If someone came over
Not having a refrigerator
She would trade the extra for something

From a neighbor
Stories were told with love and humor
I can recall a night or two
Sleep Ma Petra, sleep
We have enough to eat.

My Mom's identical twin sister, my godmother passed away when I was seven. She had two daughters who were approx. 11 and 13 years old, and we were as close as sisters.

Elizabeth P Brooks

The Wake

Transfixed, I sat motionless in a rocking chair. My eyes wide - opened frozen in wonder, yet cloaked with worry. Is this my mother? I continued to stare at the ice-box which preserved the body, kept the dead fresh from decomposition. The cover of the icebox had a large glass window so I continued to stare at the dead. This was my first wake.

The dead, brought to the house in this ice –box was to remain overnight for two or three days? Family and friends crowded the small room, paid their respects. They celebrated the life of the dead, in prayer, sobbing and wailing - a haunting cry. Some women sat on the floor and bawled. They trembled and shook their bodies. The Five Sorrowful Mysteries of the Rosary and the Litany of the Holy Spirit were chanted in the house, included was a prayer for the poor souls. "May the souls of the faithful departed, through the mercy of God, rest in peace. Amen." In this repetition of prayer, my aunt's name was called, we called her Auntie Teresa, but we prayed for the soul of Therese (her legal name) departed and in supplication, we asked "May she rest in peace. Amen."

After prayer, everyone went outside in banter and chatter for food and drink, and card games. I remained faithful to my watch, glued, to the rocking chair. I mimicked the dead, did not move. I kept watch over her familiar face; her image in the refrigerated box began to fade slowly due to condensation. Who could tell? Who? Who would know? Was this my mother's identical twin sister, or is this my mother?

Other rituals continued outside. Bottles of rum were being consumed heavily. There were bursts of bamboo over fire; amid lots of music; men and women danced and sang to rhythms unknown, drums, bongo, shango and limbo, many voices. Shirtless men wore a strip of red fabric tied around their heads with the ends hanging. This generated great excitement with stick fighting. The sticks were long and rounded. Dried bamboo sticks. The bamboo sticks were raised in attack and defense modes and they clicked and clacked. Blood was drawn from the men's heads repeatedly. The men squatted low and jump kicked up to music on individual legs. The men challenged each other with their sticks like a sword fight but this was rhythmic. The clacking sound of sticks continued and made its own music on contact as the two opponents in a ring attacked and defended with their weapons. At times one man would be sidelined because of his cracked head and blood which flowed. It was at this time another man who danced on the sideline would jump in the fray. This continued all night.

Full bodied women draped in flowing white dresses swung their hips in rhythm to spiritual songs, as they shouted, clapped, bounced and poured large goblets and cups of water. Chickens were clucking and flying about in the large backyard.

This is what I recalled of my first wake, I was seven years old. Someone told me the following day that the shango dance and bongo drums were to assist the dead in traveling to the next world.

That experience added to another degree of my trance until we returned to our home, days later. We were accompanied by two of our cousins who came to live with us because it was their mother who had died! What a relief! But there grandmother was put in what was called 'The Poor House'. My cousins were 6 and 4 years my senior. It was unfortunate that they lost their mother but they had more structure, more opportunity and even more food with us. They became our beloved sisters. We all tried to help them heal. Until one of my mom's older sisters split them apart. She wanted the younger child and my mother had to oblige because her sister who made the request was older than she. But we were still thoroughly engaged. They lived close to the Printery. In those days, I had seen quite a few times that relatives, even distant ones and sometime strangers would ask if they could have one of the children; as if they were asking for a chicken in the yard or a mango on a tree. This is consistent with the expectation and normalcy of human trade; part of the legacy of slavery. I am guilty of that also. Later in life I asked my niece to let me raise her baby. She said when he is about 10, and I asked again and she said No!

I was assured that it was not my mother who had died. I was always at her side and I heard our neighbors offer their condolences to her. I saw my mother go about her daily task of conducting our family business at Excelsior Printery.

My Family Life:

My parents had five children four girls and one boy. In essence, in the birth order I was the baby of the family. My baby sister came when I was seven years old. We lived in Fyzabad, South Trinidad. Fyzabad was a flourishing oil town then. My childhood was not perfect but a blessing from God and I was enriched by it. We were not rich or had as much as some but we had more than many. We had enough to share. We were raised by two responsible parents full of love and compassion and generosity.

We were staunch Roman Catholics and went to church every Friday to Confession. On Saturdays, we attended the children's Mass and Sunday was regular Sunday service which we could not miss because it would be a sin. On awakening, the first words on my mother's lips were, "Mercy, Mercy," while she softly tapped her chest. During the day "Hold your Peace." Do not murmur." She would advise.

Our family said "The Angelus" daily – "the angel of the Lord declared unto Mary and she was conceived by the Holy Ghost..." at 6:00, 12:00 and 6:00, I believe. That was a time to drop everything and meditate on this profound prayer at the ringing of a bell.   At church my mother's voice was the loudest in the congregation when she sang and as children, we would sneak glances at each other. She was no singer and I don't know if she knew the range of her voice but she surely worshiped her LORD.

My father and his mother were Anglicans and I remember Daddy attending church service at Easter. His church was pretty close to our house much closer than the Printery was. Our Catholic church was probably four times further and we walked. My father lost one of his brothers the same year my Mom lost her identical twin sister.   Both of them were my God-parents. My uncle had given me my last doll.

One of my aunts (an older cousin) taught herself to play the organ, in reality she must have had training earlier at the church in Diego Martin. She was our choir mistress and all of us (children, cousins and schoolmates) sang in the choir. I still recall an absolute stunning solo rendition of "Regina Caeli" for Easter by an older friend who was about 15 years old. The choir was upstairs in the balcony over the entrance of the church but not visible to the public. We faced the altar in the same direction as the congregants. But she was terrified and her fear changed her breathing which created an awesome un-believable rendition, operatic. One of the older girls rubbed her back very softly while she sang. Just to let her know she was not alone.

My eldest sister was very responsible, dutiful and stable. She as-sumed every role expected as the oldest child. She was selfless, kind and disciplined. My sister also enjoyed the companionship and wisdom of my grandmother, who was basically confined to the home. My paternal grandmother called my mother a Guarahoon, a wild Indian- disparagingly, because my Mom was not from the city. In Trinidad the Amerindians who were identified were Awaraks and Caribs. The Caribs were a fierce tribe and my grandmother would tell my Mom you are certainly not an Awarak. They were peaceful and loving. Early in the morning before my Mom went to work in the Printery, she took care of my grandmother's daily personal hygiene. My Mom would also do her laundry and at times I would assist my Mom with the laundry.

My brother was the second child and my mother's king. He was raised as such. We all loved him deeply and honored him. My cousin was my brother's age. She was delightful and taught me a lot. She and my eldest sister explored growing up together to become young women sewing or designing their own clothing. There are several funny moments of them designing a hobble and insisted to the seamstress that the bottom of the skirt should be no more than 18 inches wide. They really had to hobble to my aunt's house after the movies in embarrassment as guys followed them with cat calls.

My elder sister two years my senior, was the middle child. She was my grandmother's favorite. She was the red one. We had a contentious relationship. We fought verbally almost daily as children. I was petite and she was much taller with long limbs. Almost daily she would threaten to beat me up and my response enraged her. "Beat me up? You mean we would fight today," was my retort. I said that even though I was afraid. As adults we had some good times and the last time I saw her I really enjoyed being in her company.

The fourth child in the birth order was precocious me. I read more books than anyone we knew because of accessibility. I was intelligent, obedient, innocent and full of promise.
The fifth and last child, my little sister was loved by all and she had broken my last doll. The night she was born we all waited downstairs while the midwife and my grandmother were upstairs in the bedroom with my mother. I don't remember where Daddy was. We were not taught about the baby and the stork.

We were taught that aeroplanes brought babies. When aero-
planes went by overhead many little kids looked up at the sky
and said " Aeroplane bring a baby for me" while they jumped
up with joy. But we had passed that stage.

I got drunk at my baby sister's christening. I was seven. One of
my mother's classmates from the city whom I had never met
was my sister's godmother. She looked kind and full of pure
sweetness. She had a very soft voice. My mother was thrilled
that they united for this auspicious occasion. Auspicious was
another one of my mother's favorite words.

At the christening reception, everyone was toasting and drink-
ing in celebration of this event, the new baby. It was the first
time I felt alone. People I did not know were in my home. I
picked up a shot glass of rum without anyone being aware of
my predicament and chugged some of it down my throat. I
stumbled outside without anyone noticing except the lady with
pure sweetness. She looked at me in the eye but she did not
raise an alarm. I threw up what was left in my throat from
gagging and burning my tender chest. I slept most of the next
day. I awoke with a painful headache. But the celebration con-
tinued all weekend. I was the only one in pain.

My cousin and I became very close and I lost all tolerance for
my baby sister who had broken my last doll and my Daddy
said "You are a big girl now" Humph! I wanted that new doll
from Mr. Kistow's store, anyway. It was a beautiful Black doll.
I had never seen a Black doll before. Dad said we could not
afford it. The doll cost $22.00.

It is said that the eyes are windows to the soul, expressing gifts
of the divine, defining moments. As a child, all the dolls every-
one had were blonde, redheads and blue eyed. And all those
dolls rattled because their blue eyes had fallen into their heads.
We could not identify-it did not fit our reality. We had plenty

Elizabeth P Brooks

of babies in the family but none that looked like our dolls. Out of intrigue, the first thing that a baby or any child did with a white doll was to poke its eyes out of its socket. We no longer wanted them then. Arms and legs could be re-attached but those eyes left a gaping ugly hole displacing the staring blue oddity. They were very impersonal. There was no familiarity. It was not done out of malice but out of curiosity.

Interestingly enough the expatriates were less than the population of Trinidad citizenry. Yet, the market was flooded with white dolls. The only dolls for natives to cuddle and idolize, hold in their arms, cling to their chest, to shower love upon, sleep with, an obvious state of colonialism.

Calyposnian The Mighty Sparrow's album "Dan is the man" (in the van) declares in an award winning calypso that "The West Indian Reader, "tried to cultivate comedians, comic books made more sense. They were fictitious without pretense. The poems and lessons they write and send from England wanted to keep us in ignorance."

As a very young child there was a lesson we had to learn to read in school in our West Indian Primary Reader but it started on the page opposite a picture of a Golliwog which created terror in me, trauma, therefore I agree with the Mighty Sparrow's assessment and humor. I believe anyone blessed with some humanity would have recognized that could be traumatic to a child, unless it was deliberately positioned as an expression of power.

Where We Stood

*My oldest sister told me, my daddy used to beat
my mommy; another report was that they fought
repeatedly.*

*But I was a witness when my beloved father scooped
up my precious mother little woman that she was
and threatened to throw her over the banister.
He lifted her over to the other side indicating all
intention to drop her.*

*Bewildered, frozen in fear, I watched in awe as my
mother did not struggle showed no fear, held on nor
begged. But dared him to "throw me, throw me over,"
she said.
I did not cry or beg Daddy either. I stared.*

*Fearlessly, her arms outstretched not even a clutch,
grasp or clenched fist. She demonstrated that she
could be a living sacrifice in the presence of her
child.*

*Most probably Mommy had looked Daddy dead in
the eye. I don't know what he saw or what else he
heard but Daddy lifted my mother from the other side
and placed her gently down, on the landing where we
stood.*

*The only physical fight I witnessed. It was their last
physical fight.*

I told the above poem to BB one of my nephews and he
laughed. He said, "That's my Mommy G, throw me, throw me
over!" That is what my Mom's grandchildren called her.

My Mom managed the Printery almost full time. In the Oilfield, my Dad worked a rotating shift, so he was not always present. One of the reasons we never got a small puppy. A few times we brought a small puppy home obviously without consent and that poor puppy would cry all night while my dad had to sleep, so he could probably work the graveyard shift. Dad would make us return the puppy to our friends' homes.

If Dad had worked a regular day shift after closing time, on a Friday night he and his boys would be in the back of the Printery talking politics and drinking TDL, puncheon- white rum. I don't remember what the chaser was.

Dad did not pass his driver's license test and Mommy convinced him not to try it again. He had fallen down one Friday night, on his way home after drinking with his buddies. He rode a bike and after drinking on a Friday night when he was off, Daddy would walk that bike down a steep hill and curvy corner on a very dark street.

My Mom was one of the eldest housewives but the only one who ran a structured business. The other women who worked did ironing for single men or family laundry for the expatriates. Other enterprising women had a variety of goods to take to market to be sold.

My mother was a dedicated worker. She was a typesetter and printer, "chief cook and bottle washer." She maneuvered that pedal on the printing press in her high heels and skinny legs. She wore high heels, or wedge heels and sometimes a ballerina. She was the only woman in the neighborhood who wore high heels. We were the only business which sold any type of literature for about a radius of 12 miles. We sold comics, classics, novels, a variety of magazines, including fashion magazines and greeting cards etc. She was the first feminist I knew.

I was always at my mother's side. I remember my first task was to very delicately create the invitations in metallic gold or silver. At first, she had given me a piece of cotton, later I used a small brush to complete the task before the ink had dried to avoid creating a smudge. I also stamped the numbers on raffle tickets.

My mother embraced and was a friend to the old and the young. Mom demonstrated the power of her love of humanity consistently. She was very generous. One evening after school when I arrived at the Printery, my Mom introduced me to a young lady with two young children a girl and a boy, 2 and 4 year olds. Not quite yet school age. My mom told me to hail a taxi and to take them home with me. They had been at the Printery for hours waiting. I gathered there must have been much discussion about preparing dinner and other arrangements. We arrived home and I introduced Barbara and her children to my grandmother and others.

Barbara assumed a role that she may have been familiar with. She took charge of our household. She was a beautiful woman with a loud and hearty laugh. Later I found out that she had ran away from a very abusive husband. She was the daughter of one of my mother's schoolmates whom I had meet more than 8 years prior at my baby sister's christening. Barbara and I became very close. The only information she had, was my Mom's name the town we lived in and the name of our business Excelsior Printery. That family lived with us for about a year.

In terms of optics, this is who I am - a reflection of my Mom. One day I asked my chiropractor, "Would I be able to sashay again Doctor?" "Probably not" he said "and I don't know why you would want to."

There's no rhythm or rhyme to it. Once I sprained my left ankle and visited a podiatrist wearing 3 ½" heels. I did not know that was an oddity. Yet after living in the states for over ten years, anyone would have guessed I was an immigrant when I took my kids to Disney World wearing high heeled shoes.

One of my younger cousins walked very fast and wore high heels; when you think of her, you could add swinging arms and conjure up her image which is the identical image of my mother- a shy woman carrying herself like a movie star! But my mother had never been to a movie and we did not have TV. Her fashion magazines paid off.

Whenever I get dressed and put on high heels; one of my favorite things- I heard the sound of "pocksy tocks," the cackle of my shoe heel on solid ground- I derived great comfort and confidence when I realized I could recreate the sound my mother used to make. As a child, I can remember her asking no one in particular "Where are my Pocksy Tocks?" her high heeled shoe of the day.

One Christmas, my son and I visited one of my favorite cousins in Palm Beach (of which there are dozens of cousins) and she talked and laughed about her "Auntie Pocksy Tocks you could hear her coming," she said.

Yes, children identify with and pick up a million little things. We both derived joy and pleasure in hearing and seeing my vivacious mother and we give gratitude to that energy and circulate her love, as a blessing and gift. The show must go on - regardless of time stamp! In my generation there are a lot of powerful women in my family.

Fyzabad was a very social town. We printed all wedding invitations, raffle tickets and there were many social clubs. There were several anniversary dances, Black and White, White Rose, Evergreen, Blue Dahlia etc., The big bands from Port-of-Spain loved to come to Fyzabad to play at these events. We were invited to many events. At times, my Mom was asked to be an honorary member; to be the face of the organization and greet attendants at the door for the event.

As children, we attended several Indian weddings. Three days prior to Indian weddings, music would be heard throughout the neighborhood miles away, day and night. At the weddings, we ate roti or paratha with, curry channa, aloo and mango chutney or amchar. Water was poured on our hands for cleansing. We used our hands as utensils and we sat on the floor. Our meal was placed on a fig leaf instead of a plate.

In NYC, a friend of the family wanted everyone to come over to his home. He said we were poor but apparently had more than most. There was laughter, joy and faith. My Mom was surprised that someone wanted to invite us over. Very often she said no one invites us to their homes but everyone calls to ask if they can come over. Friends and neighbors who stayed in touch and others who found us when they migrated to NYC with our phone number in hand. They would call and ask if they could come and spend the holiday with our family, particularly at Easter and Thanksgiving. My family's place of business was like a small bus-top, even our home at the end of the day.

Enter OUR Barefoot Warrior

Uriah Buzz Butler was a preacher from Grenada who migrated to Trinidad to find work in the flourishing oilfield. He was responsible for a series of riots in Fyzabad and a Hunger March to improve working conditions, and wages. The Labor Riots in Fyzabad spread from the oilfields throughout the sugar plantations. Butler was considered the founder of the Oilfield Workers Trade Union and the labor movement throughout the Caribbean. He has since been considered a National hero. June 19th is a national holiday, Labor Day, in Trinidad, in honor of Butler. There is also a large statue of him close to where the Printery was located. In the 1970's Princess Margaret Highway was also renamed Uriah Buzz Butler Highway.

There is a corner on the way home from our place of business which I passed every day as a child. It was called Charlie King Junction. Charlie King was one of the policemen who came to arrest Butler during a mass meeting. Butler's supporters objected to his arrest, and a riot ensued. Charlie King was murdered: set on fire with paraffin and burnt alive.

There was widespread availability and use of arms by protesters during strikes at this time as no regard was given to the legality of these firearms. Thus, the police were outnumbered and outgunned in this moment. Fourteen people were killed, fifty-nine were wounded and hundreds were arrested in this horrific scene. Reinforcements were sent in under Inspector Bradburn to retrieve Corporal King's body. Bradburn was shot and killed, and the police were driven out of Fyzabad. (Nationaltrust.tt)

I accompanied my Mom on several Monday nights when she attended meetings at the OWTU hall with standing room only. At the OWTU meeting there were probably two other women in the room besides my mother, a secretary and another. The other ladies were outside conducting brisk business by sell-ing food and drinks. Their business was very productive on a Monday night. Mommy would stand up to speak and ask the speaker questions. I would slide down in my seat. It was too late to tug at her skirt. I was embarrassed that she dared to speak. These are all men here. I thought she would be quiet and listen. That's what she told me to do.

The next day, my Mom would reiterate with enthusiasm, every action, speech, vote, opposition and debate to my Dad, who was unable to attend the meeting that week because he worked the evening shift. I also remember my Mom attended several marches in support of the (OWTU) union, in her high heeled shoes. Generally we would rub her legs every night especially her "quat/cuauht." In my Mom's dialect that was the word they used for tree trunk and human legs. Nightly we would rub her calves at her request.

Elizabeth P Brooks

That Little Girl

She ran everywhere she went
she was so shy,
hid behind her mother's skirt,
she was so shy,
she would pluck her eyelashes out
when people talked about
how thick they were.

She could not stand to hear
how little she was, had pretty hair
she was so shy.

Everyday her mother stuck her head
out the door
"don't run." But off she went
out of breath. She ran all the way,
some said "'she'll definitely be late
for school today, poor thing!'"

but she was fast - so swift and
on time, almost late - close call
but she did her morning ritual
danced for her Mommy and Daddy.

Her parents watched as music took
her into another dimension.

When her Daddy worked the morning shift
she could not dance for him
but her Mommy was always there,
she danced for her
to her surprise - she sometimes
looked up, there was her Daddy,
"my relief came early today,"

he would say, so happy but so spoiled
she would pout and frown
in obvious glee, then smile
and dance, and dance and dance
then run, and run, and run
again to school that day.

That little girl, shy on the outside
but she had an internal drive
always glowing,
brave and bold on the inside.

When she danced,
she was mad with ecstasy
her body was ripe with rhythm
you could see the soul of
that little girl who still moves with
rhythm to the beat of every sound.

Back then we did not have a television set but a radio and turn-table. The top 10 or 20 countdown was on Sundays nights. The family would sit and watch me perform, dance to my fa-vorite songs. But shortly before one event my Daddy must have spanked me. Well there would be no show tonight. I was going to punish all of them. We sat and listened to the countdown one by one and my sisters and cousins were slyly amused that I would just sit still while I itched to get up and dance. They knew I could not do that for long. The countdown was almost over. But Elvis obviously must have been in the top 1 2 3. It was now a sacred ritual. I could not take it anymore. So I walked very sullenly to the adjacent bathroom door. Oh I could hear the music loud and clear and I danced in Elvis' world as he sang and danced for me. I was in ecstasy at the end of my solo performance. Then I heard the hysteric laughter – my sisters and my cousins had quietly left the living room and went to the back of the washroom and climbed up and watched me dance with joy. They knew that's why I had left the room. I was compelled to dance not for anyone but for me. My spirit was full with music. I did not need an audience. By the way on many of those nights, friends and neighbors would be in our front yard looking through our window being at the top ten countdown show.

The Dance

The emotion

    the strum

        the sound

            the chord

                The Spirit

                    the rhythm

                        the wave

                            the beat

                            the drum

                                The Spirit

The lyric

    the expression

        the body

            the freedom

                the dance

                the joy

                    of the Holy Spirit[4]

Scared by Red

My talented Auntie Desi, a dressmaker in high demand from the city, designed and made two beautiful dresses for me. One day, she asked me what my favorite color was, and I beamed as bright as the blazing sun and said, "yellow." She mentioned that she would make me a beautiful yellow dress and the other color would be a surprise.

She kept her promise. I owned the most fabulous yellow dress. It was a closely fitted dress. The fabric was a bonded jersey knit which sat on my body closely without clinging. The blouse was sleeveless and fitted at the waistline with metallic tabs which lay flat at the side. The skirt's hemline fell just above my knees. That dress made me feel like I stepped out of my mother's fashion magazines.

The other was a disaster for me; a red silk dress that everyone raved about, yet, that dress intimidated me. "Auntie Desi, How could you, a red dress? This is too much attraction and attention." I pouted. Staying true to her style, she smiled. I was coaxed into wearing that red dress on special occasions because it met everyone's expectations. It was a red evening dress with a jeweled collar, red glass beads around the high - neck and deep cut armholes: a loosely draped swing dress which ended at the top of my knees.

My aunt tried to bring me out of my shyness. I was full of humor, laughter and joy, very playful and childlike but mentally bright and I believed I was mature. But, I had always been troubled that some people interpreted my constant laughter for childishness instead of pure joy. Then again others expressed that I was too shy and unsophisticated to accept a compliment.

Back in the day, we talked about our zodiac signs. Taurus is my sign. The symbol for Taurus is the bull and I was proud of my sign and intrigued by the fact that the bull seemed proud, content and strong. He knew his place, yet he was powerful and direct in his gaze. I thought it was the most captivating and powerful sign of the zodiac. I saw two or three of these exotic bulls in a pasture daily, on my way to school. The color appeared bronze, brown or black mixed with white and the simplicity of the curved lines showed the rhythm of muscles and movement, full of grace.

I identified very strongly with the bull, with its traits and characteristics. But my vision of the matador's intention created havoc in my head. I had seen several bulls but never a matador (except in the movies or in a book). A matador wearing red would be such a threat to a bull. Falsely, I believed I had to be very careful around the color red. The color red represented danger for me. I became frightful and resisted that color which indicated blood and gore. I was so traumatized by blood, that the color red symbolized; I did not think about the fact that bulls are color blind and reacted to movement. To many bulls, matadors were non-existent. Few bulls had a matador in its reality.

Was that frightened image, the fear of red embedded in my head, from my experience with Mr. Superville? He was a neighbor who unknowingly gave me food for thought. He tarnished the innocence of my childhood. The homes in my neighborhood surrounded a large circular park; a verdant landscape, with swings and beautiful grounds and a cricket field. During the nights of full moon, we were on another planet, encased in moon glow. Our community congregated outdoors while children played games and parents roasted corn on the cob or peanuts. These moonlit nights were a big part of my community where we created fond memories. We celebrated with family, friends, food, fun, song and laughter.

One of those nights, I was wearing a pair of red shorts. The only pair of shorts I owned, then; a gift from Auntie Ruby another aunt who lived in the city. I was around 5 or 6 years old. My younger cousin liked to sit on Mr. Superville's lap when we played outside on those nights. One night, I jumped onto his luscious Santa Claus lap. I remember sucking on a stick of sugar cane and swinging my legs happily. It was then he put his fingers underneath my shorts and tried to touch my noonie, my soft spot. I jumped off immediately and never sat on his lap again. He cast an evanescent shadow though unforgettable. I assumed the burden of being vigilant until my childhood pleasures wooed me away from that shocking reveal, so vile, a pedophile. I had no idea why he did what he did and what it meant. I was a child but I knew it was not right.

I encountered Mr. Superville on another occasion. I was riding a bike on my way to visit my cousins, approximately 4 or 5 years later. He told me explicitly what he wanted to do to me. I had just learned that four letter "f…" word but I pretended I had no idea what he was talking about. (We spelt the four letter word then with the vowel "o" not "u") Besides being afraid, I was too ashamed for him. How could a grown man have no shame and speak with such a filthy mouth? I had not yet met anyone who spoke like that.[5]

In my late 20's I consciously decided to erase that fear of red which I resisted – that alarm bell in my head. I was still enamored by the strength and presence of the bull so I embraced my bull headedness, my determination, my stick-to-it-iv-ness.

I love the appeal of being in control; so it was time to deviate, become a victor and never a victim. It took courage and self- discipline. I also shared my story about that moonlit night with my family and shed my fear. My mental spirit became the curved lines, flexible. The curvature became my sensuality as a woman and transcended "my bull" into a dimension of victory.

---

5 Published in Spirit Fire Review

I had become confident and at the end of the day with all of life's challenges that I confront, by the grace of God, I am left standing.

Red is my favorite color because I am a conqueror and I make every effort to conquer my fears daily. Intimidation in my life is non-existent. When I wear red now, I'm drenched and covered in the blood of Jesus. That's what my spirit says.

Elizabeth P Brooks

Bone and Flesh

Between the ages of five and six, I spent the night at one of my relatives' home. In the middle of the night, there was indeed a rude awakening. I was introduced to a hard penis. My cousin was masturbating in/with my hand. The entire night was still, not a mouse moved, nor any sound was heard. He had an orgasm in my hand. But I thought he had bled in my hand but he was not crying or wincing in pain. My little mind was very confused. I held my hand open waiting for the break of day to see what was in my hand. Was it red from blood? Did one of those blue green veins break? It must be green, then. I was feeling sorry for him, something was definitely wrong. This thing was wet. Of course, I feel asleep but the biggest mystery was when I awoke there was nothing in my hand, no stain of blood or evidence of a broken vein. And he had gone off to work.

A Spirit That Is Alive

My eldest sister said, "We were all raped." I believe most of us were. I did not offer my body, it was taken. Some of my first cousins were virgins when they got married, particularly the twins. They were much older than we were. But my generation was a generation mostly female with limited men around to provide protection.

There is also another variable. Some of the female relatives lost their mothers at an early age. And so was my mother's generation which put them at a disadvantage, and they had become vulnerable and probably fallen to prey. I concur, we were all raped, my sisters and I and several cousins. Most of the perpetrators were not always strangers but relatives, some good friends. Others were the men we thought we loved.

We were betrayed by them! None, not one of us laid down gently into the night or backed up willingly into the wall or dirt, when we were dragged under the house or behind the shed. It was all violent and rough and we said, "No!" We resisted throughout the aggression while the men insisted that we enjoy it.

It was a lot of fuss and fussin', a push up, a pull down a back up, a turn over, roll over or throw down. We were good girls, fine young women, some of us still children. We protected these men out of love, out of shame. Out of the fact that no one would believe us, who can you trust? Everyone would continue to pretend to not know what was going on. It was a rite of passage, the men's right as they invaded our passage. Yes, and they were all men not boys. The men thought it was their right to take what they wanted. These are men who claimed they loved us or who sincerely had a deep affection for us.

Few of them would protect the innocence of the ones "they

loved." I caught myself in very precarious places and situations with my "boyfriend." I was sweet 16 and he was 23 years old. Every occasion that we were alone, I had to fight my way out. I fought and prayed to God fervently that this would not happen to me before I was eighteen at least. I wanted to have the experience as a woman not as a child. Instinctively I knew it would be wrong and misguided.

I got really close.

Elizabeth P. Brooks - Surprised by roving photographer in a private space, I grabbed his cap to hide the rollers in my hair (circa 1963)

BAM

My classmates were an exciting group during the years and we had wonderful teachers.

Mr. Ifl- was one of the exceptional ones whom everybody loved. He was very innovative. Apparently he was fascinated with my head. I clearly remember a couple of times he held my head and rubbed his hand along my hairline, my forehead and temple; (another male teacher held my head the same way) On one of those days he took a head shot of me. That was one of my favorite pictures. Now I wonder, did I like that picture because I remembered a tender moment? Maybe he was studying photography. He had tilted my head at a certain angle. He also had two very young children who had just started attending school whom we loved dearly. We were in our early teens 13-14 years old.

Mr. Ifl- decided to have our class Christmas party at his home. That had not been done before by any teacher at our school. This idea was exceptional. We were thrilled, felt very special and grown. He had the ability to make you think you were his favorite. He was a very popular teacher. Many of the older girls would drop by our class during recess to chat with him. He was very cool, tall and handsome.

During the Christmas celebration at his home we ended up in another room. He held me. I was gleefully happy, naturally. I loved him so much. Then he pulled me close towards his body and looked at me the way lover's looked at each other in the movies. I had never had a boyfriend or been kissed before. But he tried to kiss me - on my lips. I hesitated, then I almost did. But I realized he had very bad teeth so I pulled back and left the room.

Days later, I mentioned the incident to my mother. We found

out that his wife who was absent from the party was one of his prior students from another village who had become pregnant at 15. He was relatively new in our town.

Many years later, after I had migrated to NY I heard he had married one of the older students who came by our class often to chat with him. I even saw them together at a party in Brooklyn. They acted quite normal but I was taken aback by that. Later I realized that's why she showed up so often in our classroom at recess. I was able to recall and to interpret the expression she wore on her face then. She was not shy she was flustered and was trying to contain her excitement in his presence.

Switch Blade

I remembered the guy who pulled a switch blade on me one night. I was 15, and he was probably almost twice my age. He asked me repeatedly to take my pants down as he threw me down on his bed. He was unsuccessful in unzipping my pants, when he kissed me. He said he just wanted to touch me. The kiss was full of emotion. This was my first kiss and I almost believed that he just wanted to touch me. I never wondered with what? He pleaded with me and almost convinced me but I did not want him to see the big pin in my clothing. I was wearing a high-waist pair of pants with a bolero top. One of my cousin's had locked my zipper on the inside with one of my nephew's diaper pin as I instructed her to do. I never left the house without that reinforcement. That was my master card.

One of my older cousins had come to my rescue. She began to pound the door down and I rushed to the door to open it. And he challenged me with the blade extended and his forefinger on his lips commanding me to be quiet. I reached for the door lock and by God's grace I flung the door open. Apparently, we were gone for quite sometime. I was trying to convince him that we should get back while he was trying to coax me to do his will. The switch blade was still clenched in his hand. My cousin received a cut on her hand and we spent all night in cars, like a caravan outside the hospital, waiting for her to get stitches. I was very traumatized by that incident. It took about 10 years before I could talk about it. No one in my family knew or asked whether he was successful in his quest.

I was intrigued by him. I met him at Trinidad's first Independence Day celebration and he made me laugh a lot. He wrote me my first love letters and mailed them very often. His penmanship was perfect. The night of the near incident, I could not wait to get a kiss as we walked toward his door. That Boxing night (Dec 26) there was a large dance at Palm's Club. We were all there, my cousins and me. The guys however had a difficult time ordering drinks at the crowded bar and someone suggested that he, Ch- return to his house and retrieve a bottle of alcohol, to get the party started. He lived within walking distance and he had quite a stock. Everyone had quite a stock for Christmas. Someone volunteered that I accompany him. Obviously, I was thrilled (but it could have been a setup) I knew I was going to be able to get a kiss and I was excited about that. I also knew that his mother was at home, so I felt safe. We were all at his house an hour before. I did not know that she had left the house shortly after we had visited. The house was now in darkness, the walkway was pitch black. I expected him to retrieve the bottle, get a few kisses on the way back and return to the club. He had other plans. He insisted that I come into the house and I was playing cool and unafraid. I never thought that he would try to hurt me. I was really more afraid of the dark walkway where I expected to wait.

Growing up, my parents were very strict. These mishaps and close mishaps occurred away from home, when my siblings and I visited one of our favorite aunts in another town for the weekend. My cousins had more freedom than we did and they were four and six years older than me. They were street-wise and savvy and had left school early. They had inherently developed survival skills and I was a favorite cousin, who was full of innocence and very daring, full of laughter and loved to dance. The music stirred my soul and made me drunk and mad with ecstasy. My body was ripe with rhythm. You could see my soul revealed. I had to tag along no one could deny me. My eyes were wide with wonder. The first time I went to a grown-up dance, I was 12 years old, not unusual at carnival time. The person who was collecting the proceeds at the gate told my cousin, the admission fee is $3.00 per person. My cousin replied, " this one is only 12." The response, "she can come in for free."

During the time my parents were raising their first three kids some of my Mom's nieces lived with them intermittently.

Back then, if any young man wanted to date my Mom's nieces he had to write a letter of visitation to my father. There is a repetitive story of a young man showing up at our house to date one of my cousins after he had written the letter. My father asked "What are you doing at my home? The response was "Mr. Brooks didn't you get my letter of visitation?" Daddy said, " Yes but I have not yet responded to you." He asked the young man to leave and Daddy thought he was undeserving of any response after that interaction. Another one of my cousins left our house in Fyzabad to go to Diego Martin on a short trip. Three days after she had left home my father realized she had not left Fyzabad but was actually staying with her boyfriend, a man older than she. Daddy marched up to the man's house and ordered him to marry her. They were married immediately.

When I was about nine years old, my mother and I would go by late evenings when my sisters and cousins were at teen dance parties. We would arrive at intermission. My mom was really guarding the girls to make sure they did not leave the premises with a boy. I remember dancing outside many venues and someone would pass a hat and collect change. Women sold golden sweet oranges, roasted peanuts and corn on the cob outside these venues. I never received any money but one night a man bought me an orange.

Elizabeth P Brooks

My Sex Education

"Go look for your trouble." Mommy

"You can tell a lie, but your belly will tell the truth."
-Aunt from the city

Dogs, chickens and ducks

Medical Encyclopedia (1 volume) Daddy locked up in a cabinet.

When my cousins and sisters discovered that the cabinet was unlocked. The encyclopedia contained pictures of the female reproductive system and the birth canal.

An afterthought on my sex education.

On several Sunday afternoon discussions, Daddy talked about comportment; the way we should carry ourselves as young ladies. My cousins and sisters had long faces during those discussions, and I would pass by and smile at them, deliberately because I had my freedom. One Sunday, as I passed by to taunt them Daddy invited me into the meeting. He said, "you are a young lady now." I was so mad at Mommy, she told him I had my period. She said, "He is your father, he has to know." We were also told on many occasions that we should never accept a gift from a boy, not even for our birthday or Christmas. On a side note: my brother was never in on those discussions.

My First Crush Was One, Two, Three!

The power of my first love consumed me, filled me with passion and created in me an inability to choose one, two, three. Three loves wrestled for my heart simultaneously; the church, dancing and reading and writing, in no particular order of importance; even though I thought I would become a nun. I danced every day instinctively; in the rain I would dance and pretended to be a fairy. In many ways Elvis won. He was pure joy.

During Lenten season, we had to give up an indulgence for the entire 40 days. "Make a sacrifice," my Mom would say! I overhead some older guys in the neighborhood chose to stop cussin' and older men stopped drinking' alcohol or taking the Lord's name in vain. Most kids gave up candy and other sweets. I chose to stop going to the movies, unless Elvis was playing in one of the neighborhood movie theaters. I would beg and sulk pretend to cry and my mom would let me. Elvis strummed my soul and made me whole. I was never still. I danced when I breathed. One of my older cousins informed me that I could not become a dancing nun and I was stunned. That devastated me. On another occasion my cousin told me I would have to shave my head if I became a nun. That was an easy sacrifice. At that time my cousin had sewn a beautiful long sleeve dress with cuffs and a high neck for me in preparation for becoming a novitiate.

Someone asked my daddy to have me apply for an upcoming position at the courthouse. He said, "No, he did not want me to hear about those vile things that occurred and were heard, in a courthouse." My Daddy wanted to protect me. That was before!

Elizabeth P Brooks

How I Met Your Father

A newcomer appeared in the village. In my mind everyone seemed intrigued by his looks, his demeanor. No one was more handsome than he or dressed more exquisitely.

His clothing was handmade by God who dropped everything to fit and sew these selective textures of his clothing onto his perfect body. He was a living man doll. His thick thighs filled those shark-skinned pants. He was a soccer player – a goalie.

There was a small gap in the gate that surrounded the soccer field. Sometimes after school, I would steal glimpses of him on the soccer field as I walked by when his team practiced. A joyous smile spread across my heart and my little steps quickened with excitement, my lips apart in awe of his image.

He was older than my big brother, yet I loved looking at him. He was 23 and I was sweet 16 and still my Daddy's little girl. On other days after school he would pass me going in the opposite direction. He rode a bicycle that was recognizable. He had added a white thin strip to the bars, very subtle but identifiable - a touch of class. I was able to spot that bike from a great distance – sometimes outside a shop on my way home from school and my heartbeat would quicken at that now familiar pace and for a few seconds I could not breathe. I knew I was in love. My body would freeze into slow motion hoping that he would come out. Now!

Coincidentally, one day we shared a taxi and sat side by side. This impeccably dressed man with thick thighs, clean shaven and handsome, sat next to me. He did not speak except to say "Hi." We traveled the short distance in silence. The taxi dropped me off. He now knew where I lived. I got out and never looked back. Shortly thereafter, he pursued me. I was outmatched, outwitted, outsmarted, introduced to the language of wolves.

He Was No Teenager

The first time we spoke he told me he had his eyes on me, since I was 15 years old, he was 22, then. There was an upcoming Calypso show and I rode my bike to the Recreation Sports Club to purchase tickets. I did not go inside but waited and asked someone who was going in to purchase the tickets for me. He worked there as a bar-tender–a brief stint of employment of which I was unaware. I was unaware of his existence. He said, "Your breasts fascinated me." Breasts? I thought to myself, men are silly. I was flat-chested with large nipples and a bee sting full of painful sensation. My mom would very playfully say to me. Did you get stung by a bee?

He told me he wanted to kiss my breasts since then. Oh, I was grown now. I had a man's attention. I began to see him often when I walked home after school with my friends. He rode in the opposite direction about 2 or 3 times a week. He would look at me and nod his head in greeting. Very discreetly and politely, I would acknowledge him. I wanted to scream and say, "Look at him," about to lose my composure.

One of my friends said, "he has a mirror on his bike. He can see your reaction, Ms. Cool." Much later, he told me he was admiring my legs in the mirror. He was especially fond of behind my knees and upper thighs, and he loved the way I walked. He even told me I walked like a horse and tears filled my eyes and I began to walk away. And he inquired about my mood change. I said, "I'm not going to talk to you while you insult me." He then informed me he had given me a compliment, a horse is majestic, graceful, and elegant.

One Christmas night during the caroling season, he and one of his friends came to our house long after we were in bed and sang Christmas carols looking upward at the bedroom windows. We went towards the window, and I was swooning when

81

I realized who was singing. They had great singing voices. I fell in love that night. I was in my own movie. He serenaded me. It was my Romeo and Juliet moment.

I observed him at a bicycle shop obliquely opposite my family's business. We were raising funds at school for an event. I crossed the street to sell them raffle tickets. Later he told me he knew that I did that to check out his penmanship. No disappoint there! His penmanship was flawless. One day after school he stopped his bike and handed me a large Cardbury chocolate bar which I accepted. I really was not that colonized. I did not like chocolates. My breeding, my 'jam', my loyalty to my culture is spicy food, obviously Indian food; bara, doubles or phoulorie with curry channa. When he continued on his way, I would hand the impressive chocolate bar over to one of my friends who was ecstatic. Shortly after he accompanied me to the matinee on a Sunday which was another one of my rituals.

At 15, I had a boyfriend, another grown man who had kissed me and tried to put his hand under my dress. I never dated him again. We struggled and I broke the zipper on my dress. My newly designed dress which the seamstress had made for me to attend Southern Games, a grand International sporting event.

We were so colonized, wearing dresses to sporting events. An international sporting event like we were going to the races in England. We attended many international sporting events track and field and race cycling.

I owned my first pair of jeans, a black wrangler, at about that age. My sister who had migrated to England to study, to become a nurse sent us annual packages of clothing. I remember receiving a pink can-can too.

A Major Detour

God, My Holy Father has a plan for me but there was a major detour-
I met someone who attracted me
　　he corrupted me
　　　he disrespected me
　　　he shamed me
　　　　he violated me
　　　　he failed me
　　　　　he mocked me (my faith)
　　　　he embarrassed me
　　　　he threatened me
　　　　he promised me
　　　　　he disappointed me
　　　　　he exploited me
　　　　　he defiled me 2x

I wanted to be grown. I did not want to be violated. I wanted to be respected, wooed, courted, and coached.

Elizabeth P Brooks

Seduction

She had been seduced
     at a young tender age
        when emotions
           and raging hormones
              betrayed her
                and put her in the company
                  of an older man
   in the struggle she lost herself
     her veil was rent
        and her soul quaked that it
           happened to her
              she lost her virginity,
                her innocence.
her innocence
     rocked, stolen - just taken
        beaten down, beaten out, soiled,
           and without regard, discarded.
discarded
     like it did not matter
        who she was and what this child
           was called to do – to become

           to fulfill her destiny.

Pregnant Pause: Shock and Awe

My mother was my confidante. At 17, I had an abortion, and my mother knew about it. My father had gone to work, and she placed me in her bed to look after me. She looked so sad and in pain, but she was trying to protect me from seeing the pain on my daddy's face. Even though she was very upset with my boyfriend, she allowed him to come up to her bedroom to see me. She gave him privacy to visit with me. In my mother's pain, and I am sure disappointment, she showed us compassion. To my shock and horror, he wanted to have sex with me then. He said he was not going to enter me just rub against me. He insisted it was going to be safe even though I was having terrible cramps and bleeding. I was resisting quietly, too afraid and ashamed to let anyone know about his intention.

My grandmother was in the bedroom next door, but she had a stroke and could not get up. However, my mom could come back upstairs at any time. So, I cried. He showed no compassion. He never put anyone above himself. His need for sexual gratification had surpassed decency. It was all-natural instinct, all about him. We never spoke about that incident. As mature and as sophisticated as we think we might be, many of us never recognize abuse, physical, sexual, and emotional.

Elizabeth P Brooks

A Mother So Tender

A mother
so
tender

Hurt and
disappointed mother
who kept your secret

A mother so tender
gave you her
bed to recuperate

Hopefully heal,
as you
bled in your body and
spirit from the abortion
you've had

Hoping she would
not tell your Dad
to break his trust
and heart

You pray fervently
as you both bled grievously
in hope and prayer
to be forgiven and healed

in your body
mind
and
spirit.

Say What NOW!

At 18, I had a beautiful baby girl as an unwed teenage mother, and high school dropout. My baby's daddy was unemployed, with no skills or training, no intention of going to technical school to learn a trade. Some of the young men in the village went to technical school to gain an apprenticeship in the oilfields, as electricians and welders. They were gainfully employed. Others even younger obtained driver's licenses to conduct taxis. They were very enterprising. Even some of the apprentices owned and drove taxis. Others played music and formed orchestras. These young men rehearsed daily to improve their skill.

I became very disillusioned with him, and the love began to fade or become impure. I did not want him to touch me. He had promised me that we would be OK, that he would load a truck if he had to - to take care of us. His broken promise awakened a spirit of resentment within me. That was a deep sense of betrayal, the fact that he did not load a truck, and did not keep his word. That would have been admirable. It would have shown character. I would have gained respect and looked up to him because he was trying. He proudly brought a container of milk weekly for the baby probably for the first year of her life. I don't think it was even in a bag. His sister most likely was the one who contributed to that. He never took care of me or had to take care of us.

Unknowingly, my parents had visited his parents to discuss my pregnancy and his intention. Well, his father spoke for him and said, "the boy (25 years old) was not working and could not take care of a wife and child." I could only imagine how heart-broken my parents must have been. But it was true. Meanwhile, I had seen other girls in the same predicament as me and the boys' family took responsibility and or made sure that the boys did. This is when the truck loading position should have been applied for and filled. I would have been truly proud of him even though he thought that position was beneath him. That would have been a true demonstration of sacrifice for family. He would have been the man, but would I have been his wife? We would have been a family then.

That broken promise was a big ache in my heart, and I wanted to hurt him back. I felt devalued. The truth is, I did not want to get married. I thought I would be the favorite aunt to fuss over my nephews and nieces. I did want him to have the decency make an attempt to make things right, to be a man. He did not even have an instinct to give the baby his last name. No pride there. No sense of connection to family or sense of responsibility. He could not take a stand so there was no peace or purpose, but he was full of physical passion which denoted his criteria for being a man.

The truth was he was offering nothing different than any other man as a matter of fact, much less. He did not stand out to me because his vision was limited. Besides which, I was a young girl who had lost every opportunity that was available to me at the time, to have a successful future. I was a high school dropout. I was unaware of the significance of my plight. I was ecstatic to be pregnant and expecting a baby like it was a toy. All my friends in school were happy for me because everyone knew I wanted a baby, no reality. For quite some time, I pretended I was pregnant and it was a joke with my friends. I was unaware of the consequences and not as mature as I thought I was. I was playing doll house. I had not replaced that broken doll with the black doll from Mr. K's store.

My first nephew arrived when I was 12 and the second one when I was 13 years old. I was very diligent in giving care to the second one. I was very responsible as a caregiver. My parents had hired a chauffeur and sent me along to bring my sister and her baby home. He was about three weeks old, I placed him on my lap during the long drive back and hired myself as his babysitter. I fixed his formula, changed his diaper, and washed his laundry. The times I went to a teen dance party I would put him to sleep before I left the house, or worry all evening about whether he had fallen asleep yet. One of my sisters would be mad and would suggest that I stay home the next time since I am worried about the baby.

Elizabeth P Brooks

Teen Naivete

A brand-new aunt! My first nephew, one of three was born and I was ecstatic. I showered love, affection and care on them all. With anticipation, I looked forward to having my own baby; as if it were a toy. At age eighteen, I became pregnant and full of joy. Anticipation turned to fear with the impending delivery date. When my contractions began, I was in denial. I had contractions for two days and kept it a secret. Luckily, one of my cousins noticed that I disappeared every 20 minutes and found me bundled over in pain. The decision was made to call the midwife who insisted I come to the facility immediately.

My family had located a private facility where a dedicated registered nurse and midwife had turned her beautiful home into a retreat for birthing babies. This was a very private facility where upper middle-class women were pampered. I was not one of them, obviously. At this home, women would bring babies into this world with dignity, joy, and utmost respect. My family did not want me to go to the government hospital where I would be scolded, and/or reprimanded by critical nurses and staff who would most likely make crass jokes about engaging in sexual activity at such an early age.

I arrived at noon, accompanied by one of my cousins. I was received by the midwife and her staff, and they began to prep me for this auspicious occasion. By that time, the contractions had become closer. The midwife said there was no time to give me an enema. The baby would be here shortly. I was asked about the amniotic sac "when did my water break?" I had no idea or experience of a water break, or oozing any fluid. I remember hearing the term "dry labor."

After several hours, the contractions were coming hard and fast, very intense but the baby was not moving down as expected. I was given an enema after all. The baby appeared to be stuck, the delivery had become complicated. The obstetrician on standby was called. Intervention was needed. Meanwhile I was crying out due to intense back pain and I was tired of lying on my back. The doctor arrived at 10:30 pm. But with the skill and care provided by Nurse Lal and her staff, my baby arrived at 10:25 pm, five minutes before the doctor arrived. Everyone was relieved. The baby was dark red, almost purple in color, yet magenta. My baby was a girl. The umbilical cord was wrapped around her neck and her hand was up, possibly why she was stuck. She was in a fight. She was gasping for breath and sticking her tongue out. All attention was on the baby now, I heard my baby cry. She was full term and weighed 5lbs.

Then more contractions began. I screamed "is there another baby? "I was informed it was the placenta. My midwife examined me and my placenta was delivered within twenty minutes. One of the nurses sponged my face making sure I felt cool and refreshed. My mother had told me to ask for the placenta, but I did not.

My baby was put on my chest, and we snuggled. This was my baby, my very own. My baby and I were left alone for a few minutes before the midwife returned.

Elizabeth P Brooks

THIS IS WHAT I AM COMPELLED TO TELL

**Now I know I will walk
in the manifestation of my healing!**

LIVING IN A FALLEN WORLD

BOOM TO BOOMERANG

I SPEAK TO MY DIGNITY

MY COURAGE

BEARING MY SECRET

THAT WITHOUT A NAME

NO LABEL

COULD NOT BE DEFINED

NOW

I SPEAK BOLDLY

FOR MY CLEANSING AND MY HEALING

FROM SHAME AND BLAME

WHICH HARNESSED MY SPIRIT

LEFT ME

INSULATED

ISOLATED

Elizabeth P Brooks

BOOM

No one knows the secret contained in the depths of my soul. It still haunts me. This secret could still break many apart. Others could be devastated because I dared to give voice to what I witnessed. But I choose to no longer carry the burden and pain within.

I hear the whispers, the blame "Good God" the yelling. "A 60-year-old secret is better off dead and buried." "No" I scream echoing the profound silence in my mind. I have carried this weight, this burden far too long. I need to be healed.

I unveiled this secret today to celebrate my freedom my dignity. I reclaimed the power of my psychological posture. I refuse to be a mosaic of a victim culture, once voiceless.

Now I speak

To be free of guilt, shame, and fear of blame
that stripped me of my identity
who I was meant to be
I need to shed my tears
to be cleansed
for my healing.

Mercy & Truth are met together
righteousness and peace have kissed each other (PS 85:10)

Elizabeth P Brooks

Survivor: Breast Buds and Bunk Beds

At a Writer's retreat, I was invited to be a human book at the Human Library session. The theme of my session was "Survivor." I added a subtitle "Breast Buds and Bunk Beds." Now I have to be accountable to tell my grave secret because of the subtitle. There is no turning back. My entire life I did not want to categorize my experience, to name it into existence; instead in my head I minimized it and made excuses for it.

They called my brother a mathematician. He graduated from a prestigious college at age 17 and accepted a job offer at a college as a mathematician. After one summer break he was propelled into the status of manhood. He taught students who were older than he. His role evolved into something which was a great challenge to his newfound status.

I never heard my parents complain but my brother began to stay out late on weekends at the sports club with older men. He indulged in playing card games which were prohibited in our home. He also attended late night movies at movie theaters. When he returned home at night, he never came upstairs to the bedrooms. He slept downstairs. This was another sign of his growth and independence. He was earning his keep and had a prestigious position, especially for a boy. He was at the top in a man's game.

I took the opportunity to promote myself, sleep at the top of the bunk bed, in his vacant spot. I was flying high and basking. But my self-promotion was short lived. My tongue could not scream my voice was not heard; my throat did not rattle a gargle. Like a thief in the night, my brother came to steal my joy and my light. He rocked my horizontal throne in an effort to dethrone me. He had introduced me to betrayal and deceit. I was awakened. My brother was playing with my breasts, my breast buds. I was 11 years old, obedient, and innocent; Daddy's little girl. It was a thrust, a push, off my pedestal which deflected my spirit of trust and love. In the dead and silent night, I could hear his spirit shout, "Who do you think you are? You are nobody!"

Grief dotted my heart, sunk into my marrow and seeped into my soul. But my soul wouldn't die. It shivered and wobbled. I felt like a toad. But "God allowed me to maintain the integrity of my heart" (PS 78:72). Where am I? When did this start? Where else did he touch? Will anyone save me? I embodied a deceptive and deceitful stance. I lay there still like I was the treacherous snake in the grass while he was free to exploit my body. Who is the victim here? In a fight to hold onto my spirit, in my silent scream for help, suddenly a sound escaped my lips. I'm not a corpse, no vulture will pray on me. I interrupted my breathing. Every battle has a cost! My body stirred and he stopped playing with my breasts.

I kept guard knowing I could not succumb to sleep; he is a viper. Would he strike again? He had just injected venom into our relationship. That herd of silence trampled over my skin. I did not want to shame him. I could not break my mother's heart. She was our rock. My mother grounded us in the essence of her love. In my parent's eyes I was the perfect child, full of promise, so this has to be unspoken. But is this the norm? I cannot allow my light to be dimmed. At that point of my life, it was my intention to become a nun. I prayed and asked God, "Am I defiled?

I left the top of the bunk bed and never infiltrated enemy territory again. He had shattered my foundation. I soaked my pillow and washed it in my tears (PS 6:6).

Elizabeth P Brooks

Boomerang

This was advantage. I felt violated, humiliated, confused. It was wrong and I wondered why or what I had done to be scarred like this. Discarded! My spirit was always on the outside looking in. How can I give voice to my pain? Who can I trust? I had no support system, and he had no shame or concern for my welfare. He had dishonored the family and never apologized to me. Did he think it was right? But this is home. Isn't home supposed to be a safe place, a sanctuary, filled with trust and love? He did not conform to family norms. This is taboo, unexpected behavior but he had experienced power at an early age.

This was a dark season. I had discovered and tasted the stench of betrayal. This was my pit. As a child, I became a cactus planted in a desert with spines and prickly thorns which enabled me to keep a safe distance. I became self-sufficient and independent. A bruised reed will never break (Matthew 12:20). Victory was already won. I learned to be content. I never asked for anything. Sometimes when my dad was drinking with his buddies and getting soused, he would say to me "You never ask for anything. You are so contented. Take this!" He would empty his pockets. I was a child with a great disposition. I loved everyone. He was the alpha male, but I was alpha female, alpha everything.

As a cactus, I am succulent and can contribute many gifts to humanity because I am spiritually enriched. God didn't let the devil steal my joy. I have the ability to survive and grow in times of lack or excess, drought, rain, and flood. But I watched everyone around him. They were tall trees in his forest, stable with deep roots, unlike me. They enjoyed rustling leaves and boisterous wind in his company; to everyone he was larger than life with quite a reputation, as a womanizer, yet it was believed he was faithful to family and many friends.

Incidentally, my oldest sister jokingly recounted often, the audacity of my father who came home one day with two pairs of shoes for one child and at that time there were four kids in the family. I remember gleefully how I sung my feet which echoed Daddy's smile. These shoes were exquisite. They were neither black, brown nor white. One was midnight blue and the other oxblood in color, both of them patent leather. I was the child whose father had bought her shoes of many colors. I loved my new precious colorful shoes because the gift was a beautiful surprise from my Daddy.

As a 13-year-old, those shoes were worn and long gone when I saw the horror of a pig being slaughtered in my neighborhood. I was carrying one of my nephews on my hip and he also witnessed it; that brief encounter. Sometime later, during Christmas dinner my nephew refused to eat a piece of ham. He could have barely spoken but he said "piggy". I thought he was too young to realize what he had witnessed. Then I realized that baby was traumatized. He has never ever eaten pork.

My sister also mentioned on several occasions that I was Daddy's favorite child. I disagreed. I insisted it was my baby sister who was his favorite. She finally convinced me when she mentioned, "Well, If Daddy had money, we would have had to kill you." Joke!

That day of the BOOM sound within my spirit, I cast my crown to the ground. (Rev 4:10-11) I am a faithful child. I worship You Lord. I give You praise, honor and glory. As I grew older the secret controlled my relationship with my family. I created physical boundaries for my protection. It took me in and out of their lives. I still could not tell anyone, could not trust anyone. That little girl still shuddered inside. They will find and make a way to betray me. I know the flesh is weak. Their secrets have already been told but that did not diminish my joy.

When I shared my story, at the HL session, a woman at one of our tables asked me, "How did that incident shape your life?" I was stunned by the question but in an instant the response washed over me. My family is very clannish, but one of my sister's mentioned that she told her boss "I stray" when he had inquired, why did I leave them all, in NYC including my parents and relocated to California with my two young kids after my divorce and I did not know anyone there. I was surprised by that revelation but then, it seemed like I could only trust myself. On reflection, I realized I had always moved away from the state, town, county and yes, country we call home. I yearn to be safe and free. I sacrificed my relationship with them to ease my remnant of bitterness, deep pain, and powerlessness, as a child. I just want to experience bliss. I love them dearly and forgive them for things "unknown" and bless them. When we are together, we celebrate each other. But no one knows the spirit that drives me. I had learned to carry my heavy burden!

I have learned to be adaptable in various settings and have contributed to positive change in environments. I am resilient, true to myself, and comfortable in my own skin. I know it is all about character. I continue to share God's joy and laughter.

Despite that threat or let me restate, the molestation (now I put a label on it) from boy wonder, I am the first generation graduate from a scholar's program who pursued and completed a Bachelor's degree with great distinction and a graduate degree. My dad's voice still rings in my ear, loud and clear as a bell. I hear his mantra, "You are my horse and I'm betting on you." I was planted on solid ground. I know who I am. I am somebody filled with God's goodness and showered by His grace. God has kept His promise to my parents. Without a plan, I continue to be surrounded by books, print, audio, or digital information to promote lifelong learning. This gives the community equal access to information and empowerment for the public good.

With HIS own hands God stitched into me threads of persistence, resiliency, and knots of boldness to sustain me. I never truly stifled, swallowed or doubted my identity. I walk through open doors or more importantly open doors appear before me. God has showered me with Divine favor, daily. I know who I am a child of victory and everyday God shows me how much He loves me. Very often during the day I ask, with a beaming smile "God how come you love me so much?"

1995 graduation, at age 48, receiving a Bachelor of Arts (magna cum laude) CUNY Lehman College Scholar Bronx NY. Degree in Sociology.

Elizabeth P Brooks

Smoke & Mirrors

As a newcomer in Los Angeles, I met a young man named J- at the credit union office and he wanted to introduce me to one of his friends, C--. I was a newly divorced mother with two young children. I was awkward at dating and 3K miles away from my home and my family in NY. The last thing I was looking for was a relationship, however I met C- sometime later. We all worked at the same lot and would eat at the commissary sometimes, so we ran into each other. C- and J- introduced me to the trendy "In and Out" burger joint, which was close to my house. J- lived in Los Angeles and C not too far from me. They both met my kids, one of my girlfriends and one of my visiting sisters. The guys visited me a few times after work and brought hamburgers over. J- dreaded getting on the freeway in rush hour traffic but C- lived in the town adjacent to me. C- and I began to develop an affection for each other. We had gone to see a play together. I met him at the Pantages Theatre in Hollywood. I did not realize that I had built a reputation for not going out with a man unless I could take my kids.

One day, I had car trouble and could not get to work. I had already discovered that there was no hailing a taxi in the valley, like in NYC. My first thought was to call C-. We were getting closer, but I decided against it. I did not want him to think this was a clandestine moment. In my zest to get to work and to get paid, I called my friend J- and made him aware of my situation. He decided to rescue me.

That was a cloak and dagger moment. He came on to me unexpectedly after I opened the door to let him in and turned around to pick up my purse. He grabbed me from behind and pushed me. I was pinned against the wall, his pin-up girl. J- was a big guy and I was about 20lbs lighter than I am now and he caught me of guard and over-powered me. I stopped struggling not believing this was happening. But he had a great imagination. In a split second his business was done. Barely any interaction, besides being beyond vile and he had absolutely committed a crime.

This feeling wreaked of familiarity. I was enraged and felt undermined, belittled, and diminished. Broken! I was livid and cursed him out though I had no words for it. He said, "You know I have always wanted you." By the way J- was married and I don't remember an apology either.

I pretended nothing happened because this was sheer madness. Ironic! He dropped me off to work and I saw him many times after. The same pattern continued grabbing some burgers and coming over with C- like there was no betrayal of trust. C- was dumbfounded that our relationship never got off the ground. I sacrificed my relationship with C- because of guilt and shame. I never told C- what happened.

The vagina is very sacred, a hidden treasure full of mystery and secrecy- from conception and birth. It is mesmerizing and spellbinding. It also has the ability to morph into and take on stages of power to powerlessness. It is not just an appendage but truly is a bouquet layered with silk and satin bows and petals. Some men are very threatened by our innate strength and ability to develop coping skills and really thrive. They try to erase the mystery and its beauty. I am reminded of my ex-husband. He wanted to be a part of the complete structure, the elasticity, the flexibility. He wanted to own the sensation, the lubrication, the warmth and 'supap' (one of the words from my mother's tongue) of my vagina. He would attack it with so much intensity as if his intention were to remove it, to take it away. He wanted to master it, to conquer it; like he was trying to get a trophy to hang on the wall but very often I would reveal to him, "You cannot kill this you know."

Elizabeth P Brooks

Poetry Stayed

My church rejected me then Elvis left me. I read a lot and I loved to write, so poetry was the one who stayed.

The first poem I had written for the school's newspaper, was published when I was in third grade. The title was "A Song for Jesus." I can still see my teacher's joy when he brought the newspaper to the class to show me that my poem was published. I couldn't see it. He kept saying "Right here, look!" I couldn't see it. I was not looking for my name but the title which he had changed to "An Ode to Christmas." I was devastated. My teacher did not recognize my relationship with Jesus. My poem was for Jesus not for Christmas. My poem was personal. I knew the difference between Jesus and Christmas then. Besides which, I did not like or know the word ode. The message I received from his decision; I was not good enough. It was published because he changed the title. This was his poem.

It would have been wise if he had mentioned it previously - as a teaching moment to introduce me to the word ode. When I was asked to give my testimony at church it was revealed to me that no one can take my gift away from me, but it is my decision to use it. As I mentioned previously the title of that poem in my Women's group "Beautiful" was so named in celebration of women's dignity. With that revelation I had a clear picture of me acting like a graffiti artist claiming territory and painting my expression boldly. I renamed my poem "We are Beautiful" to "You May Applaud Now" without any apology or embarrassment. That act did not require permission, or more importantly, it was the re-identification of that child in third grade claiming her right and the ability to write poetry.

My middle name was Odette. One of my teachers in an earlier grade often greeted me with a smile on his face when he said, "O death where is thy sting." He thought that was funny.

104

I thought that was cruel. Hence the word ode was offensive to me.

It probably is the reason why my poems are filled with emotion. Poetry allows me to breathe and thrive and become fully alive. It compels me to listen to the voice of my soul, to suppress fear and negativity. Poetry allows me to raise my consciousness and spread inner beauty and an outward look toward humanity.

Elizabeth P Brooks

Some Silly Moments

Poetry my love, I still don't know much about you except I love to be with you, preferably in bed. And I love to talk about you. I derive great pleasure as you explore my heart bursting with desire and my soul with fire. Yet, I know little more than before.

I am free, open and receptive, a lover of good and fine, like my hair no longer thick. I fell in love deeply, long, and hard with you. You have me Poetry, in the palm of your hand. If I play with my tongue, I can call you Pretty, pwetty, poetry.

I have no desire to indulge in the conventional and be part of the ritual and trappings of who you are. I am me. Do not conform. Yet, still flexible because I am inspired to grow though sometimes rigid. I refuse to be bent and twisted anymore.

In the midst of joy and great laughter, my friend CAM and I decided that when I share and talk about my love for you and my heart's desire, she would explain my what, and my why. She accepts all the challenges of poetry to the nth degree.

The Celestial Heavens

God has a great big band
the Great I am

My life reflects
The celestial heavens
melodious

A little blues, hip hop
some reggae

On certain days
Maybe tomorrow
Some soulful cries

A little soca, salsa n' chutney
gospel, merengue
waltz, tango, and disco

That's what I see when I look up
at the clouds and skies.

Everyday it's different but I see the parallel with the 12 disciples of Jesus and the 12 tribes of Israel. Supposedly one of the biblical meanings of the number 12 denotes God's power and authority, perfection.

Oh, thirsty mercy filled with longing.

Elizabeth P Brooks

An Empty Chair at the Table

Cosmopolitan Trinidad and Tobago, my homeland, had achieved a milestone and became an Independent nation. That transition labeled us a Third World country instead of a British Colony. It was a time of hope, promise and possibilities. Opportunity was ripe for those who had an education, but the unemployment rate was still very high. Many citizens intended to emigrate. It was a painful process to obtain a passport in Trinidad and Tobago to pursue the challenge of emigrating. Money and favors might have been traded. Many people wanted to obtain a visa of any type to migrate to the States, which meant showing a large bank account. The passport office had very long lines and people had to return several times, after standing in line all day, so I have heard. Before daybreak, people assembled in line at the United States Embassy daily, with hopes of securing a visa. Unlike many around me, obtaining a passport to emigrate from Trinidad was not in my cerebral hemisphere. Life for me was joyous and happy, living day to day.

Because I was noticeably pregnant, I could not sit my final exams. My life had become stagnant. My prospects were dim. But I had the joy and love of a close family, my baby, my parents, siblings, dozens of close cousins, and friends. But my life was unfolding. There is always a turning point "He brought me forth also into a large place: He delivered me, because He delighted in me" II Samuel 22-20 (KJV). God showed me that he would always provide for me. Miraculously, one of my older cousins who lived in the States, dialed a wrong number, and she was asked if she knew anyone who was looking for work. God put my name on my cousin's tongue. She gave the prospective employer my name and address in Trinidad. There were other cousins' names that she could have given, her peers, but she didn't. Like manna from heaven. I received a letter from my prospective employer and was advised to take it to the

US Embassy, immediately. I was going to America to work, to be a foreign maid in Long Island, New York. I was informed that I would have to work at least eight months or a year to obtain my green card. I left my close-knit family and beautiful two year old baby, everything I knew and loved and made me who I was, to come to a strange and foreign land. That decision to migrate came out of a desperate need to have a future. I embraced the opportunity so that I could provide for me and my tribe. I became the hope and the dream.

Within three months, my travel documents were finalized. I stayed in Diego Martin, the edge of the city, during that time; with my eldest sister who had returned home on a visit from England, my baby and me. We had a friend who owned a car and was instrumental in driving us around to the various government offices to save time, money, contain the excitement and reduce stress. He had a great sense of humor. RA worked at a newspaper publication in the city. God spoke to my storm. I never encountered any incredibly long lines at the passport office or US Embassy. I went about my business, smoothly. Of all the people in my world who had intentions to emigrate and spoke about their prospects, suddenly, I was the first one who left home to migrate to the States. My sister decided to travel with me on her return to England, to give me moral support. Seven years prior, she had gone through the throes of uncertainty and anxiety when she migrated to England, leaving two babies behind. The positive lining in her walk of faith was that she went to join the love of her life.

Baby's daddy and his friend advised me with some insistence that I return home within one year to marry him so he could migrate to the US. With great humor, subtle threats were made obviously emotional blackmail, on more than one occasion, that I probably would never see my baby girl again. Obviously, I had to leave her back home. I was coming to America to work to be a foreign maid in Long Island, New York for $50.00 weekly.

My father paid a considerable amount of money to purchase my airline ticket and to have a dressmaker design some winter clothing for me. I was going to arrive in New York City in the month of March. My Mom bought an expensive piece of gold jewelry for my boyfriend to present to me as I was about to migrate. She handed him an embossed gold slave band (so named because of the size and weight imitating slave shackle) in my presence and said "Give it to her. You cannot let her leave without anything" (someone had to tell him that). He took it from Mom and handed it to me without any rhythm, not even tic tack toe just robotic. He did not express any emotion like it were an entitlement. He gave it to me, and I felt ashamed for him. He never offered to pay Mom back and I know she never received a penny from him. My mother was not perfect, but she was the perfect mother because she was mine. I think she tried to give him hints of how to treat me, how to be a man. My mother will always be my shero.

During my departure at Piarco Airport, several people came to say goodbye. Meanwhile, my heart was throbbing. My sister suspected my turmoil and my friend RA- knew what was going on deep within. I had vocalized to him that I don't think I could get on that plane to leave my baby behind. I said that throughout the entire process of paperwork. Now, it was time to board the plane and one of my sisters used her womanly wiles and proceeded to walk towards the gate, with my baby. She got beyond certain checkpoints. The challenge for me was to stand at the top of the stairs of the plane and wave goodbye or bolt back down. I kept thinking of the disappointment that would be to Dad; the prohibitive cost and loss to him; he would be distraught and disappointed in me if I didn't board the plane. Earlier that day, he had said to me " Remember now you are an ambassador; when you get there represent your country well." Then I replayed in my head, what he had always said, since I was a little girl, "You are my horse, and I am betting on you." My father in heaven blessed me with an earthly father who has always spoken life into me. His statement declared to me that there is always hope and a future for me. I reminisce on that sweet refrain ringing in my ear, I smile, and I say owner, trainer, rider even after my father had been long gone. I smile and I say, "Dad we won." It is like having my very own daddy and daughter dance when the spirit moves me.

Time to climb the steps of the plane and my friend climbed too...my sister and I were so confused...He was still escorting us, holding on to my carry-on luggage. Climbing the stairs, I was now in crisis mode, descend or wave. We found out then, that RA had a plane ticket to Barbados, the first leg of my flight and we were ushered in quickly. What friendship! He knew how difficult my choice was. He was brilliant and had such sensitivity and insight for a young man. He was only 21. RA did that to distract me, to secure my future. "God is my strength and power: and He maketh my way perfect. He maketh my feet like hinds' feet: and setteth me upon my high places" II Samuel 22:33-34 (KJV). RA- and I corresponded

March 1968 - Mommy at Piarco Airport

with each other for fifteen months. It gave me great joy hearing from him. I read his letters to my cousins which brought immense joy and laughter. I never saw him again.

I arrived in NYC in the dead of winter March 30th, at JFK Airport. My cousins met me with a winter coat, and we took a taxi to my new residence in Washington Heights. I wanted to write instead I gazed out of the window of the plane. The concrete jungle was sprawling and spiraling. Nothing was familiar and everything looked as cold as it felt. We spoke about getting acclimated and familiar with riding the New York subway and the Long Island Railroad by the end of my first week. At that time, I should call my employer to let her know that I had arrived and was ready for work.

On day two, my cousin handed me my first piece of mail. Everyone was stunned when I opened it. We all screamed and did a dance. This was a gift from God, a miracle, my green card in my possession.

After my arrival, on April 2nd we witnessed in shock, the horror on television of the assassination of Dr. Martin Luther King Jr. The violence, riots and fear erupted in cities, and I listened over and over to "I Have a Dream" speech as tears rolled down my cheeks. My world had changed forever. About 10 days later, we visited the Audubon Ballroom, in our neighborhood; the location where Malcolm X was assassinated.

My America

At age 20,
when I arrived in NYC
my new American friend
told me, "if you ever have a son tell him
not to run, he will be shot down.

This is America. Black boys can't run."
Shocked, I opened my mouth wide
threw my head back and I
laughed at that, our eyes locked.

I remember being ignorant
of such a fact.

But this was no joke, no folk tale, no lie,
no phantom cry
my friend had relayed a warning
like a message beating on a drum
about a deviant human condition
abnormal behavior - human to human-
like a cannibal - an American custom.

He said if you ever have a son
tell him not to run. This is America. He will
be shot down. I replayed in my head
what my friend said.

Later I recognized, This IS America!

If he runs he is guilty, guilty of
something yet to be concocted
or not yet determined.

I discovered that it really does not matter

Elizabeth P Brooks

whether you are a son or daughter, mother
or father the common denominator
is color. If you are black, you can be shot
down to the ground by any policeman.

Police brutality comes from anyone in Blue,
male, female or persons of color, too
because they have been trained by others
who devalue you. To many their actions
are not vile but vital.

Instinctively, they want to eradicate you.

Two weeks later, I called my prospective employer and told her that I had arrived. She gave me directions on how to travel by the LIRR and said she would pick me up at the train station. I met Mrs. S who greeted me very warmly, but she was taken aback because I looked so young. I arrived at her beautiful sprawling ranch home, and she introduced me to her husband and daughter. There were two other children who were away at college. She also gave me a tour of the elaborate house and added that she had prepared my room; and I must remember that I am part of the family. My cousins had advised me to travel very lightly. I arrived in my cold room in the dimly lit basement and noted the bathroom was on the opposite side. The basement was not only lit dimly but on the drab side. There was an old metal file cabinet in my room and I asked about that and she just pooh pooed and waved her hand.

We had already discussed my chores. Cleaning the house daily and doing laundry. In my country, my family paid someone to do laundry and cook for our family. My mother cooked on Sundays. My experience in ironing was to iron the pleats on my school uniform skirt, nightly. I returned upstairs for dinner and Mrs. S served me a plate and I ate at the kitchen counter, while her family ate at the kitchen table. Lie #1. I was part of the family. I was eating at the kitchen counter and there is an

114

empty chair at the kitchen table. She gave me a pile of linen to change my bedding. Had she not prepared the room for me? Lie #2. After doing dishes, I returned to the not very lit basement, took a shower, shivered, changed my linen, and proceeded to go to bed. There was a radio in my room. It was the first time I remember hearing the hit song, "Cry like a baby." I cried like a baby, nightly. "My eye trickleth down and ceased not without any intermission. "til the Lord looked down and behind from heaven, Mine eye affecteth mine heart because of all the daughters of the city." Lamentations (3:48-51 KJV) That song played every night and I filled America, this cold country with more of my hot tears. I wondered what my baby was doing. What was she thinking happened to me? Where was my Mommy? This was a gigantic sacrifice. I fell asleep when I became numb and empty.

Cleaning was my specialty. I love a clean house. My sisters used to say, I had obsessive behavior in cleaning. It was the first time I used spray starch; the result was professional. My employer was pleased with my work. I felt safe during the daytime even though previously, I had never been alone. During dinner, Mrs. S could not contain her excitement about Thanksgiving. She wanted her friends to meet me. By the end of the first week, Mr. S had come into my room after 10 o'clock at night to retrieve a file that was in his filing cabinet. He knocked at the door very softly while he called my name. He had a beautiful office upstairs, yet a filing cabinet in my room. That was very disconcerting. I was terrified, and afraid to sleep that night. This reeked of familiarity of my cousins' stories. Based on their experiences, I realized travel lightly was a metaphor for you may have to run and leave your belongings behind. Initially, I thought it meant I did not have to take too much clothing since I was going to be wearing a French maid uniform.

After the first week of employment, Mrs. S paid me less than agreed upon. I was stunned! She claimed she ran short of money, but informed me however that she had to deduct some money to put into a fund in the event I became ill. It was for my protection, she said. The 2nd and 3rd weeks she claimed she was short of money again. My family determined that she could not afford a foreign maid. She had breached her contract with U.S. Immigration. My green card was already delivered before my arrival in the US, at my residence, unknowingly to her, for such a time as this. God gave me an opportunity and He made sure no one could take that away from me. He also gave us free will and Mrs. S- wanted cheap labor, cheaper. That was the status quo, exploitative! She treated me like I was undeserving. Her choice was not guided by the Spirit of God. This was injustice and white advantage. Her actions were tainted; not very subtle, recognizable as if it were a zit on a new born baby's face..

My stint of employment was three weeks, and I did what was required of me for the position for which I was hired. I never returned to her home, and she never called to inquire about me. Probably it was her intention to drive me away. Her husband had continued to return to my room, once a week to retrieve documents at 10 pm way past my bedtime. I did not have to make compromises, God had honored my sacrifice. My situation was unique because generally the green card went to the employer's residence and was held as a bargaining chip, or submission whip, sometimes. At moments when I might have been fearful or doubtful, I prayed a prayer my mother taught us all. Living on a prayer and The Magnificat (Luke 1:46-55) which magnified the presence of the Lord; I knew then that all would be well. "For God has not given us a spirit of fear; but of power, and of love, and a sound mind." II Timothy 1:7 (KJV)

Call Who Founding Father

*We have built this country
with our backs, bent, lashed
pickin' cotton.*

*Stripped of our decency, our dignity
stripped of our religion, our family,
stripped of our language,
culture and homeland, our heritage
and our freedom, stripped of the God we knew,
the God we prayed to, and the God we
called on. Everything was taken from us
so we could build your economy,
this country.*

*Yet you berate us,
you say we are lazy, incapable, incompetent
but we made you, made you rich - slaveholder,
founding father, corporate owner, oppressor.
You use me, abuse me,
misuse me, painfully exploit me.*

*We have been stripped beaten, hanged
on a tree, left for other slaves to see
how many hundred years has it been?
You perpetuate your false sense of superiority.
Now we are beaten filmed, killed in the street
left uncovered not even a sheet.*

Elizabeth P Brooks

Who is a savage?

Look at the reflection in the mirror. It is you.
Shameful, disgraceful, without a conscience.
And my heart is like a drum, skin stretched
to the limit, beating like a battle march drum
but to survive I improvise and go inside and
listen to my rhythm - march
of a warrior woman. I am woke!
Black Lives Matter.

My Reflection on Immigration

The perceived humanity and decency of the giver
in the transaction of sponsoring a worker
to obtain a green card- an alien, an assumed beggar-
has nothing to do with humanity or dignity;
to become a legal alien part of the workforce
of the fabric of society - the American Dream-

The completed transaction of sponsoring
a worker could be a deceptive game of
vulnerability and criminality. Yet no one discusses
the two-fold part of the employer - the taking –
the unexpected illegal transaction.

My sponsor was coaching me for something illicit-
He knew better. He was an attorney.

Why was his weekly visit to my room after 10 pm? Was his wife asleep by then? Or was that part of the coaching that I would trust him, ultimately leave the door unlocked for his convenience and just stay in bed while he retrieved his document.

Did his wife think I was having an affair with him? Is that why she never paid me the salary she agreed upon - As my sponsor she robbed me every week- (and she was a school teacher) and also deducted money for SSI- or medical insurance, she said-WOW!

Within a couple of weeks, I went to an employment agency and was given an aptitude test for data entry knowledge and efficiency. Immediately, I was hired by a brokerage firm, on Wall Street. My first job on Wall Street was at Winslou Cohu and Stetson, 26 Broadway.

I could not stand having an entire hour for lunch. I thought it was a waste of time. Especially not knowing the area, what to do, nor where to go, (I had not yet discovered Century 21 Department store which was a hole in the wall then.) Besides I thrived on eating one meal a day, unless it was my dhal, bhaji, phoulrie and doubles. Even a roti or dhalpourie was too much food for me. I was a finger foodie, a nibbler.

At lunch, I was sitting at Bowling Green Park, and I had half a sandwich for lunch enjoying the greenery in the middle of Wall Street area, being homesick. My eyes popped open and I began to hear familiar music in my ear, a steel orchestra. This infectious music was playing, and I sat there like a tourist; until my numbed body began to walk like a zombie toward the sound. Outside the building where I worked was (British West Indies Airways) BWIA Sun Jets on a truck. This was a Springtime concert on Wall Street. I was delighted and I knew a few of the players. This musical band rehearsed close to one of my aunts' homes in Trinidad. Many of their fans would go by to listen to their rehearsals. One of my aunts' nephews was one of the musicians.

I danced to the infectious music of my culture with wild abandon. I walked around the truck which was stationary. I waved to some of the guys who recognized me. I had just left home. This was a popular band with many fans. The sponsor realized that I was familiar with the band and I was asked to come on stage and show the audience how to dance to this music. The spirit filled my soul. I obliged willingly. I had a blast! We exchanged phone numbers and I was asked to go on tour with the band. (I did not go on tour my aunt said 'No".) After this brief concert which was worthy of every lunch hour. I returned to work. At work, everyone exclaimed that they saw me dance. They said "We had no idea the new quiet girl was so brave and could dance like that." When I dance there is no space, distance, or time.

I remember when my eldest sister migrated to England to study nursing. She asked Daddy to send me to England to study under Trinidad's renaissance man, Boscoe Holder; the elder brother of Geoffrey Holder who was a great dancer and choreographer on Broadway, New York. My father asked me if I wanted to migrate to England and I told him that I wanted to go to Hollywood. I was about 13 or 14 years old at the time. My father proceeded to tell me about the casting couch in Hollywood. At the age of 9, I had already performed as a dancer on stage in an adjacent town. I was the youngest member in a dance troupe. I remember the excitement at the community center when we rehearsed several times a week. I was also the lead actress in a comedy drama and performed to a standing room only in the school drama festival representing our county, St Patrick. We qualified to compete with several counties but were finally eliminated.

I derive a huge thrill at the Fearless Girl bronze statue on Wall Street, right in front of 26 Broadway where I danced during my lunch break, at a street summer concert. I was newly hired to work at a stock brokerage firm. I felt this statue was commissioned for me a young immigrant woman. It represents me after my immigration story, where my sponsor had all intention to do something illicit with me. Both subjects the Fearless Girl and the Charging Bull encompass who I am a defiant bullheaded bronze girl with a charging spirit. In my bullheadedness, I am challenging and confronting the bull. That beguiled stench which can squelch good intention of immigration and reveal other forms of oppression. The statue was strategically placed in honor of International Women's Day. I have a copy of that bold image on canvas. It is a Christmas present from my son. I'm a conqueror through Christ who loves me. Hallelujah! Look at Me! God supplies all my needs according to HIS riches and glory (Phil 4:19).

I had a solid educational background. I was always at the top of my class. I just did not have a certificate to show I was a high school graduate. But excellence was in me. I always assumed positions of responsibility at work. My cousin was the instrument God used to challenge the system to light my path. In the midst of the emptiness, culture shock and assimilation, I arrived at a status which enabled me to build structure for my family. I began to save money so I could sponsor them. I had to have a savings account with a qualified amount to show the US Embassy I could take care of my family and not be a burden to the system. I remember the Christmas when I opened a savings account at a bank on 34th Street and Broadway. I deposited $25.00. The branch manager said to me "Do you know how fortunate you are to be opening a savings account on Christmas Eve, when most people are spending their last dollar? That gave me hope!

Fifteen months later, I returned to Trinidad to marry my baby's father which enabled me to sponsor him and my daughter. It was an intimate ceremony in San Fernando. We got married in the same church where Mom and Dad got married and where both my daughter and I were christened. We honeymooned in my beautiful beloved Tobago. I was running out of time, but I had to see my friend RA. On the last day of my visit, I went to his place of employment to see him. I longed to see my friend. Unfortunately, he was not at work and no one knew when he would return and I waited but was shattered. On my return to NY, I wrote him a letter and informed him that I came by to visit him and was so sorry that I missed him. His response was that he was there looking at me. He did not want to see me. How could you return home to get married, when I loved you? I was shocked. He had never told me that. Two letters trickled between us after that. I lost my loyal, beloved, and ambitious friend who made me laugh a lot. What if I had known that he loved me?

I got to Hollywood in my late twenties after my divorce. I was being stifled in my marriage. I worked at Universal Studios in the basement of the strikingly imposing black tower; as a data entry operator. The basement housed the mainframe computers and all the accoutrements designed to empower "the tower" to accomplish and fulfill visions, create the magic of visual storytelling and immense profitability. The black tower housed the offices of the executives. This is where they discovered talent, fulfilled dreams and created careers.

One day in the middle of my shift, my manager answered the phone and told me the call was for me. Taking personal calls in the middle of the shift was frowned upon, however I took the call and the person on the other end invited me to dance in an upcoming movie, "Xanadu." I asked "how do you know that I love to dance?" His response was "by the way you walk." I could not carry on this personal conversation in my manager's presence. Obviously, I was shocked, taken aback, but I responded in a very casual tone and asked him to call me back at three o'clock, during my break time. Obviously he did not call back. He had given me his name and I should have said or asked can I call you back on my break at 3:00pm? That opportunity to dance in Hollywood died a natural death. We were very busy and worked at a hectic pace. We ate at the commissary often and saw all the important people and we were invited to many wrap parties. It was a fascinating place to work.

Yet, I resigned from my position. I was tired of working with machinery. I felt like I was becoming a machine; everything was too automated. I wanted to develop some of my personal skills; work with people. I went to Snelling & Snelling Employment Agency in hope of finding a sales trainee position because I had no sales experience. After being interviewed, management at Snelling & Snelling determined that I was a good fit to staff the vacant Sales position as a recruiter for their company. I was trained for my position by the owner and the month I went live as a Sales Recruiter I earned the award for top recruiter. I hired sales people for Fortune 500 companies like IBM etc., Management from other companies tried to steal me off the desk. I had placed and earned more money for the company that month and made more money than I ever did.

After I had married my baby's daddy shortly after a year's time as he "prophesied" I sponsored him and my daughter so that they could migrate and join me in NYC. But after the wedding I discovered that I was pregnant. The immigration paperwork was getting tedious, and I was getting very frustrated and tired. I had a husband who was unable, emotionally incapable, and unwilling to help. Ambitious young men and young women, friends and relatives were migrating to the U.S. on a visitor's visa but he had no inclination to do so. He was a saga boy, manipulative, coasting in life. He had a sense of entitlement. Undoubtedly, his value was elevated due to the color of his light skin and good hair. But his letters kept coming with insinuations. Interestingly, my mom had said you don't have to marry him he is already like family.

There was a terrible snowstorm in NY and my company asked me to stay home. Do not return to work. Now I was unemployed with rent to pay, medical bills, food, preparation for the baby. I had to pay the hospital $800.00 before the baby's due date. I was now seven months pregnant. I had the last straw. I had to come up with a strategy. I devised one. A Western Union telegram to him stating "Elizabeth critically ill, wants to see her family." The original document is dated Feb 26 which I still have in my possession. (My daughter calls me the Elizabethsonian.) They had to come immediately, or the marriage would be over. My oldest sister was afraid that such a desperate and urgent act would come true. But she sent the telegram for me out of my need to come to a resolution.

The American Embassy gave my husband three days to leave

the country. He came without my child. He left my daughter behind. The telegram did not suggest or imply but clearly stated "Elizabeth critically ill, wants to see her family." Once again in glaring headlight, there is no vision. He arrived the week before my son was born.

The night my son was born we had gone to the movies and returned home and was awakened by contractions. We went to the hospital together by cab and he returned home. He did not have the need, instinct, or urgency to be there in the waiting room while I was in labor. My son was born early next morning and I called the house to inform my husband and my sister that I had delivered a baby boy.

Reluctantly and embarrassed I had moved in with my sister and her husband, after my mother cried and begged me to do so. Encouraged by my aunt, I did. They were afraid and worried about me. I was now 22 years old expecting my 2nd child and still looked like I was 17 years old and alone. Some people at work did not believe I was married.

Elizabeth P Brooks

Saturday Night at the Movies

My newly minted husband, father of my first and unborn child had arrived in New York a week before my son's birth. We had our first NY date at the movies and immediately after we returned home, my contractions began, around 9:30 pm. We took a taxi and arrived at Columbia Presbyterian Hospital, within ten minutes and I was checked in.

Contractions were hard and fast, and I was taken to the delivery room. This was a renowned teaching hospital.   Yet, I was very disturbed because every doctor who came into the room examined me, vaginally. It appeared to be more than four, it could have been possibly six of them. I was in severe pain and irritated. The doctors had determined that the contractions were there but the baby's descent was not sufficient. I had severe back pain and wanted to turn on my side. My back felt like it was open and had no bone to support it. But I was told, "You are having a baby you can't turn on your side." Meanwhile, the doctor decided I should have an epidural. He explained to me that I have to be still to avoid paralysis, it will be done around my spinal cord, he said. How can I remain still while I am wincing in extreme pain? I asked myself.

Hours were going by, and the contractions and pain did not diminish. The epidural dosage was inadequate. I was given two more doses and the pain did not lessen any, nor did the baby advance adequately. During one of the many invasive examinations, one of the doctors obviously, a young intern, removed his hand and asked, what's this? Someone answered membrane. It looked like a plastic bag to me.

I felt a sensation, and I was told to push. I pushed in anguish. The doctors were all engaged with the process. Now this was unmistakably time to push again. And I asked "push?" In unison they answered, 'No". I realized then the doctor was removing my baby with forceps and had conducted an episiotomy, a surgical cut, from my vagina down to my anus, then I was stitched up. I heard my baby cry, and was told, it's a boy. He weighed 7 lbs. and 3 oz. It was 6:05 am Sunday morning. I held my baby boy and I wanted to fall fast asleep.

My doctor advised me in order to avoid complicated problems "Do not get pregnant again, within a two year interval. He said my pelvis was too narrow." I recalled why the doctor who attended to me in the clinic during my pregnancy had threatened to put me in the hospital. He thought I was gaining too much weight and the baby was getting too big. During this pregnancy I really enjoyed and indulged in eating food for the first time in my life.

For quite some time, the indentations of the forceps were visible on my baby's forehead and temple. This situation had become untenable. Two weeks after my son was born, I was out pounding the pavement daily, in search of employment, to be able to ensure that I could continue to provide for the four of us. Another one of my sisters had arrived two weeks after my son was born. We used the windowsill and the fire escape as a refrigerator.

MG, a friend of my husband invited us to stay with him in a one-bedroom apartment in Brooklyn. We moved out of my sister's apartment five or six weeks after my son was born. Fortunately, I was gainfully employed by then. My sister who had newly arrived in NYC moved in with a friend and she began to work shortly after also.

My husband's very generous friend gave him a $50.00 bill weekly so he could pull something out of his pocket, to contribute to his family. I worked the evening shift on Wall Street and returned home at 1:30 am. My husband finally found a job in a factory in Queens, and he worked during the daytime so one of us was always available to take care of the baby.

We slept on a fold-out sofa, and the baby grew out of the bassinet and playpen. Though I worked at night and arrived home in the wee hours of the morning, I had to be discreet and get up very early to recreate the living room atmosphere and not an inhospitable environment. Besides I needed privacy. The time arrived when we began to live as a nuclear family. After being at that residence with his friend for 7 months, I advised my husband that this is no way to raise a family. I need to have a good night's sleep in my own bed and my son needs to have his own room. Besides which, I added, sometimes MG's bed appeared very tempting. That last statement motivated my husband, and we found a beautiful apartment with every criteria I needed to raise a family. Plus, it was very close to the subway which made it safe and convenient for me, since I worked at night and worked a lot of overtime.

One day my husband told me that he had to sully my reputation. "I pretended we were sleeping together because my reputation was at stake." He continued "no one could have known you resisted me for so long." You see in his mind he was irresistible. He claimed he had a woman on every corner. He added that one of my previous "boyfriends" who was three years my senior had told him "she is a hard nut to crack."
Gees Louise! Everyone is a comedian! The guy who tried to kiss me while he was eating cake. When I ran all the way home, my boyfriend?" He did not have a nutcracker. He was 11 years old. I screamed inside, "Dear God, where were YOU?"

I Speak to the Sound of My Cry

*I speak to the sound of my cry and try to stifle it
inside, but the sound has pain of its own;
unable to breathe, it wrestles to be free looking for
opportunities and possibilities.
And with a gasp and a grunt, it storms through my
soul and dissed me.*

*My bones are creaking, out of joint. My outer layer
distressed like denim, my skin shredded like wheat. I
am left abandoned and mute.
The sound of my cry reverberates around the world,
in agony - frantic.*

*It's lost in darkness, searching for peace, comfort
and freedom. Tortured and blinded, it screams and
shrieks.
But like a trail on a comet's tail - Hopeful and
faithful, I speak boldly to the obstacles it encounters
as it bounces off, bruised and broken. It sends
shock waves through the atmosphere, combustion of
lightning and thunder, drought, and unclean water.*

*I speak to the scorching sun in torrid lands, the
celestial moon that reflects light and soothes the
night. I speak to the beasts that lie in wait and lie
awake to plot my demise and out of hate make me
pay a price.*

*Expended, finally my cry has weathered the storm.
Still, I speak - but in a quiet prayer to the whispering
breeze my cry has become - begging it not to roar,
soar or rustle anymore, in attempts to quench fear
and dissipate. I speak to the oceans far and wide and
rising tide: To the mountains that watch and wait*

then swallow what it wants as the valley chews the crumbs while I hunger for peace and joy.

"Please hear my cry, Sweet Jesus," I scream, as I surrender, and a shower of missiles appear and I step into a spray from above. The sound of my cry tumbles down.

I catch my breath, and we become one; a balm of cleansing tears comforts me and washes all my pain away, as I finally give voice to the sound of
MY CRY!!

Daughters of Our Cities

In urban towns and rural villages
we celebrate you!

The spirit of God dwells in you.
You may be broken but not forgotten.
Violated.

Powerful and innocent women, girls,
mothers and others who are struggling.
Deceived.

Sacrificed, enslaved, branded and
exploited because of power and greed.
Trafficked.

Daughters of our cities
We see your purity of heart
your innocence, your disheveled
beauty.

Don't give up hope. Rethink your position.
We are all grounded and planted with
purpose by God to eliminate darkness.

You are growing deep roots to bear fruit.
Daughters of our cities
Jesus Christ
has already paid a price for you,
He paid with His life because of God's
Love.

God created you. He has a plan for
You. You will be empowered.
God created you for Victory.

Elizabeth P Brooks

He will reveal the birth of your vision,
Daughters of our cities.

Espadrille and Sand

Should I have come?
am I still needed?
Does she want me?

There she is, looking forlorn
but I'm hypnotized
look at her gorgeous feet
white foam breaking, spraying,
water trickling through
those wiggly toes feet wet
and dry, stained with the shadow
of receding water,
amid sunbaked seashells

It was only yesterday
we were walking along the beach
together, on sugar white granules
and she wanted to walk barefoot
we stopped.

She held me
twirled her fingers, swung me around
full of laughter
until she dropped me, unknowingly
in the sand and I was suddenly washed away
I am the color of a haunting sunset
with hues of blue
her beautiful espadrille shoe.

Elizabeth P Brooks

Finding Myself Through My Hair

As far back as I can recall, my hands became very tired when I attempted to comb my hair. This was a tedious process for long kinky hair. It was the untangling of "an unruly mop of hair." Yet, everyone played with my hair, and my friends at school tried to braid it neatly, when I arrived there. I was very petite as a child. When the elderly looked at me, they said "Her hair is just sucking her dry."

My beloved mother had little skills in styling hair, particularly the challenge on my head. Several comb handles broke during the act. She was a busy woman with a business to run. At times, she would chop my hair down to my scalp at certain spots, to thin it out. It would ease her dainty wrist from the struggle. When I tried to comb my hair into two braids, I would encounter the stubbles hidden between the tresses from which my mother had chopped. My paternal grandmother suggested that we obtain a comb that is used to comb a horse's tail. The shape was curved without a handle and was grasped in the palm of the hand and able to resist pressure from combing through long, kinky hair.

One Saturday, my parents were expecting me at our place of business, to run an errand for my mom. My errand was always to go to the market to select a pair of earrings for her. I washed my hair that Saturday and I was home alone. After deep concern about my delay, my father returned home to see what had happened. I was in tears. I could not untangle my hair. There was no hair conditioner. My dad combed my hair very tenderly that day. He showed me how to part my hair gently into sections, to minimize tugs, pulls and breakage.

Several times, my mother had my hair straightened for the purpose of manageability. My hair was independent and resisted being changed. It had a life of its own and it fought against being tamed. After each straightening, the new growth of hair became more robust, and we finally surrendered to its victory. At eighteen, I exercised my will and opted for short hair. That did not please many people. The length of my hair should have been a source of pride as it usually is for most women. One of my favorite aunts told me, "Now you will sound like every black girl who says I used to have long hair." But I was in control of my hair and the way it looked. It was straightened, short and manageable. Because of the density of my hair, I was asked very often if I were wearing a wig.

During my early twenties, in New York City, I wore my hair in an afro style. I let it be, no conformity. I was in love with my hair and my hair was in love with me. This was my halo, a statement of black pride, joy, happiness and acceptance of self and I loved my image. My husband also wore an afro, but he suggested that I should trim mine, for the sake of employability. He felt my afro was too much of an "in your face" statement. That would have curbed my style. Another obsession with my hair, hah! My afro was voluminous. People even asked then whether I was wearing an afro wig. Much later, I conceded to expectations, though deep down I wanted to go bald, but some were appalled. I fell into the pack of straightening my hair again. A small fortune and considerable time was spent at beauty shops though I enjoyed every bit of it then.

I rebelled again and embraced wearing my hair in dreadlocks for about six years. I was surprised and amused while on vacation in Tobago, a vendor on the beach addressed me as "Rasta woman." I moaned with ethnic pleasure. It has been 20 years since I liberated myself and decided not to spend valuable time and money straightening my hair. My hair is about shoulder length, longer if I blow it out. I am much older now. My hair is very thin at the top, still natural but pulled back in a bun at the nape of my neck, sometimes a little higher up. Some people are still obsessed and want to see how long my hair is. "Why don't you wear your hair open and not pulled back?" "How long is your hair?" "You should wear it down!" I smile sweetly, knowing, I will no longer subscribe to insanity. That was such a farce, compromising my beautiful natural hair to meet the expectations of others. I do not struggle with my blackness. I am a deeply fulfilled black woman. I am me. Unapologetic![6]

Elizabeth P Brooks - Me and my beloved halo.
No conformity. April 1970

---

6 A version published in Huffington Post and Spirit Fire Review

Unapologetically ME

Clearly actions and repetitions
define the standards of beauty

As a result, the surgeons of the rich
and the obsessed carve my regal pout
into the look they crave

They fill out the desired pucker
to their mouths
and with collagen give definition
to delineate the thick in their lips

Their need to create the contour
of my rock steady butt –

My thickstride of thighs and rolling hips
dictate unapologetically

I am the natural and original woman-

Their obsession could be a yearning
for the DNA mapping of their matrilineal
lineage to Africa

Many things that are hated are recreated
consciously or unconsciously-

But they can't RECREATE my resiliency
it is not a collective-

My resiliency was uniquely designed
by my Master's hand with purpose
with me in mind.

I am one-of-a-kind

Elizabeth P Brooks

I cling to HIM in reverence and awe-

*I praise HIM on my knees with extended arms
and open palm, I SURRENDER- daily.*

Unapologetically ME![7]

No need to twist and modify African American women's hair-style. Don't co-op my Bantu knots and divine dreadlocks. Your disdain and arrogance for my dreadlocks propelled me into projecting a posture without fear. My dreadlocks style is symbolic of the tribe of the Lion of Judah. That posture emanated from deep within and I represented one who has triumphed and is worthy.

I find colonize to be such a vile concept that became a living thing. It is justification for committing crimes. The word colonize is morally wrong. It was motivated by power and greed. Deceptive promises like a carrot and a stick and student loans. "Student loans " is one of my pet peeves, I owe $84k in student loans and have never been in default. The reward and punishment for cooperation. A scam! [8]

Rebellious Wife

After being together for 11 years he said, "he raised me" and he bragged about that. My father raised me, a beautiful, well-bred child, whom this grown man corrupted. He defiled that child and that child became a woman and with all the goodness in her heart, rebelled against him. He never kept a promise, but he always earned his keep. Yes, he had a job. Those broken promises were kept in little pieces in her heart. She worked 9, 10 and 12 hour shifts at night to fill the needs of the family while he was at home with the kids watching every highly rated show on television. I don't know if he ever read a book then. He read newspapers though.

The next day the kids would tell me about Sonny and Cher, and their mommy was Cher. Daddy had a mustache like Sonny, so I had to be Cher because I wore long dresses at home and danced all the time. In the midst of all my challenges I still carried joy in my heart and spirit. On weekends as family entertainment, my family would watch me perform. My daughter emulated me. We did not need applause, as the laughter and music were the blessing.

Our home was full of music, and I would dance to everything. One day my husband said to me "You wash the dishes with so much pride, but do you have to dance while you are doing it?" Yet often he tried to snuggle up behind me for a quickie. Even if we were playing cards (I rarely played) and I had to shuffle the deck, he thought that was a quickie break. All of that was becoming old. Whenever the phone rang and our friends heard the music, they knew that he was cooking, and they would come over. We always had company and seldom went anywhere except to my mother's house. We seldom went to a movie, never a show, obviously never to church. I cannot recall seeing a movie in a theatre as a family, even though the theatre was only a short walking distance from our home.

But I started to grow up, to outgrow this man when I discovered that I had more than physical needs, obviously. I had to plan for my family. He showed no initiative. The discontent in my heart grew. I would have serious conversations with him about what we needed to do as a family, specifically what we needed from him as a husband and a father. This high school dropout felt this is what a professor must feel like lecturing to a classroom. The more I spoke to him, the more insight was revealed to me. I was full of disdain because I began to feel like I was wearing the pants in this relationship. I even told him if I wanted another child, I would have one. I did not want that.

This is why I was attracted to an older man and not a teenager. My father was solid, stable. This was very unsettling especially when we could not come to an agreement. Or better still we came to certain agreements, but he never followed through. Once we made love that night all bets were off. In his mind, that was all it was truly about discussing our needs and goals and he would agree with me. He would say "You are a genius; I never think of things like that until you bring it up." "Let us make some changes". And six weeks later we would be having the same conversation because no changes were implemented on his part. This became a regular occurrence.

Even though initially, he did not have a green card to work, he had a docket number for employment. He gained this through my calls and visits to the Catholic Immigration Agency on 14th Street. In essence, that was his work permit. His child was an American citizen, and he had a right to work. And he chose to work in a factory. I also have original documentation of correspondence to members of Congress, Congresswoman Shirley Chisholm and Emmanuel Celler seeking assistance to expedite the process of obtaining his green card. That was completed successfully. That created satisfaction within him but no impulse for upward mobility. Nothing changed.

I took action and informed him of a decision I had made, the sacrifice to open a bank account to save $45.00 through a weekly deduction. I worked a lot of over-time, and this was through the Christmas club plan and by October we would receive about $2300. We had a great New Year's Eve party at our home with many friends which became an annual tradition. I worked on New Year's Eve and at midnight I was still at work. If we were lucky, we might get off at 1:00 am. The party was my idea because I wanted a place to go to on New Year's Eve. I would return home any time before 2:00 am and the party would be in full swing.

My entire family would be there including my mom and dad. The party became a standard and I realized we had to adjust. I asked him to join a Christmas club for $5.00 weekly and when he cashed his check, he could make his deposit. He did not have the luxury, convenience that I had with automatic deposit. His savings would be the Christmas budget and mine would be our annual savings. He thought it was a fabulous idea, but he never followed through with that either. True to fashion and my culture, my children got everything they wanted and needed. He thought it was a bit too much. He said he had never received a toy as a child. At Christmas time, everything in our home was new to welcome the new baby Jesus that is, new sheets, bedspreads, bathroom, and kitchens towels. New bathrobes and pj's for the entire family.

One Christmas morning, my eyes flooded as I groaned when I arrived home after 7:00 am and the kids had already opened all their gifts. He thought giving all those gifts to the kids were senseless. One would think he would have had the presence of mind to encourage them to hold on to one gift by telling them your mom would be here any minute and she would love to be part of the surprise to see your joy.

He told the kids I was crying over my job.

The only thing that was incomplete for the big event was the (un)painted walls he had not completed. One year my husband said he was going to start painting the apartment in October, so he would be finished by Christmas. Even preparations for the big annual New Year's Eve party did not motivate him to complete it. The painting was never completed. He would say with pride I can do a lot of things, but I seldom complete anything. The truth is, he also said he loved to paint. He was very creative and mechanically inclined. When he did something, it was very well done, and he bragged about it. One Christmas morning surprisingly he had bought me a beautiful diamond ring. I was ecstatic. Two days later he asked me for the money he had spent. I gave it to him. Sometime after our divorce I gave the ring to my daughter.

He created a "remote control" (extension cord with an on and off switch for the TV in the bedroom.) He also created an alarm intruder system at the front door to the lobby and an "on and off switch" for the front door when we did not want to be disturbed. Anyone could ring that bell all day from the lobby and we would never know. When all his friends came by, he had to demonstrate the alarm sound system, every time. I begged him not to do that. The neighbors would never know if there were a real issue, besides which he was disturbing them. It is an alarm for God's sake. What I said did not mean anything. He had to show off and his friends loved to see his excitement when he bragged. His friends laughed when they gave him a pass for not lying but, declared he just exaggerated. He also introduced marijuana and cocaine into our home. He brought me a "spliff" and I had no interest. He never touched it, but he told me it would increase my appetite. I tried it a few times and had hearty meals but I did not like it. To me it was a depressant. I just wanted to sleep so I had no appreciation for it. That most likely could have been his motive.

No one was asked to bring a dish and or a bottle and no one took the initiative. However, some of our male friends would take over the kitchen and cook some fabulous meals. I remember some of our friends telling me "I should ask people to bring a bottle." I never asked and they never did. It was our party. I wanted to have some fun. I was tired of working those long hours and sleeping in the day with my baby pounding my back and wanting me to watch every Sesame Street show with him, frame by frame. He was a genius. There were several reruns, and he knew every line. After a while he understood and he would wake me, open my eyes literally only when the commercials came on. He knew I liked them.

As a family, they escorted me to the subway station on my way to work daily. My husband, "poor guy" would have to come straight home from work, really hustle to stay with the kids. We would walk to the subway station, and we all stayed on the platform talking and laughing, this was our life and lifestyle. When we heard the train coming or saw the headlight of the train around the bend, I kissed my family goodbye and inserted my token in the slot and hopped on the train to Wall Street, a relatively short ride. When I arrived at Wall Street and got off the train I had to walk obliquely opposite the subway station to the building in which I worked. That was the only place I went without my husband. Yet, continually, I was accused of having extra martial affairs. I never mentioned to him that I was not the one who bragged about the "art of a quickie." Much later I called him a quickie monster. Our friends would say "he must be doing something why does he have to accuse you, all the time." The art of projection; but some say he had the ability to be kind and attentive and raved about me. I paid no attention to hearsay which I still hear today. He does not know that his secrets have already been told, even with pictures.

His obsession with distrusting me and making constant accusations continued. I told him several times if you continue to give me that name, I will certainly enjoy the game. This was a time of protest. I wanted out. I decided to look for a place for me and my kids. It was difficult and expensive. I decided that he should move instead of three people being displaced. He said he did not have any money to do so. I gave him a contribution of $500.00 to find a place and he took it. My husband was disappointed at my mother's response when he called a family meeting, unknown to me, to discuss the state of our marriage; a "Talk to her meeting, she wants out of the marriage." Everyone had something to say while I cried, and they waited for an explanation from me. I didn't want to belittle my husband with my explanation. I cried and cried and cried.

My mother's only advice, "You have the iron in your hand, and you know how hot it is." I understood Mommy's reasoning, rooted in her mother's pain and guilt. Mama had intervened in one of her sisters' marriages and had compelled them to make up. Even though the couple stayed together, the brother-in-law lost an eye in a subsequent fight.

I was emotionally drained. I walked out of my job one night, as a result I was technically fired. But my work ethic and character were respected and honored. A person from human resources called me at home and wanted to talk about the abandonment of my job. I told her I was too tired to talk and she said she had time and wanted to listen. I was offered my position back. But I did not return to work for quite some time. I finally figured out the stress at home was more intense than at work. At one point I asked him for his contribution towards the home and he gave me $20.00. I am very remorseful about what I did with it. I told him that is the kind of change you get from a friend who may be trying to help in a situation. In the meantime, he found my secret bank account which took a lot of effort on my part to generate some security. He was always digging and searching and eying my "drawers" and bags. He moved out a year later when he realized I was serious. My bank account was almost depleted and sexual intimacy for me was bland, nonexistent. I advised him to take some time and get his business in order. I made it clear that he did not have to pay child support until then. I made that decision based on faith because I had not yet returned to work. I had no income. I know my character and that of my father. My father was a great provider, not in quantity of dollars but in determination and character as a breadwinner. My parents were consistent. "One monkey can't stop a show."

He came by very often and I cannot recall him bringing any surprises or gifts for the kids. I was too obsessed with my dream of returning to school to further my education.

During our marriage when he realized that I was considering going to college to get a Bachelor's degree. He almost had a fit. He accused me of wanting to be like Angela Davis. He suggested that I go to a school for a shorter period of time...like 6-9 months. He even had some of his friends in on the discussion of how difficult it would be to live off one salary, if I went to college. I aborted the idea because of all the negativity. In my heart however, my desire to get a college education flourished. The best kept secret I ever had.

I am an active American citizen. My entire family calls beloved America home. My baby, my parents, my sisters, my nephews and niece, many more dozens of cousins all migrated to America, and we continue to contribute to our adopted home, as productive citizens. We have a rich heritage and know that we can be competitive on a world stage, given the opportunity. We are fortunate enough to recognize the value and privilege of diversity.

Twenty years later, after my children were grown, I sat for the GED exam and earned high scores. I went to college and was placed in the scholar's program at my university without any remedial work needed. After my first semester I was placed in a writer's tutoring program. I graduated with high honors, and it was determined I should be on the CUNY Graduate Pipeline Program. I went on to graduate school. Empowering others and providing them with access to information is my cause. I believe deep within my bones that not one of us is disposable. My job is to celebrate life while pleading for justice for humanity, knowing full well that justice is essential to peace, law, and order; without empathy there will be no unity.

Unbridled Potential

A remarkable opportunity
which reveals beauty and strength
Unbridled potential reflected from
within little ole me
manifested as distinctive and exotic
steadfast and mysterious
focused in solitude
perked ear listening
to that small voice
eye showing determination
full of intent, as I experience
being in the Presence.
Image defined. On water
as natural as solid ground.

I feel the power and magnitude
of the burning sensation of
my passion,
the boldness of my vision
is sometimes threatened
with tension as I transition
because others are not able to see
what has been revealed to me
the brilliance of my talent
the beauty of my gift
that the world eagerly awaits

I am very blessed, encouraged
and fortunate
that my purpose has been
made clear to me
though sometimes elusive
when confronted with challenges
I know what I am entrusted to do.

Elizabeth P Brooks

I have the choice to recede or blend in.
But for now, my audience
is quite selective
It is an audience
of one, my protector,
provider, and life-giver.

He is counting on me to
utilize my full potential
to use the gifts He has given me.[9]

Stolen Moments

*Even now, I feel
your embrace
and savor our
every moment
your every touch
with every fiber
of my being,*

*I know
that I should suppress
what I feel
yet I resist nothing*

*I indulge all my sensation
as I reminisce about
the silence the stillness
the sweetness
of our secret garden*[10]

Elizabeth P Brooks

The Joy of Text

My nakedness
upon your chest
tender nipples and
swollen breasts
breasts, ready for you.

Responsive to your
fingertips and palm
sweet lips and gentle touch
my breasts surrender
surrender to you

I caress them
and sigh- deeply-
deeply with longing-
longing for you
all of you![11]

Still Difficult to Talk About

Sweet Memories written on scrap paper. It is over and done with- that is -the life that we knew. What is left is PURE MEMORIES, beautiful memories, treasured memories; like the sound of her laughter ringing in my ear or echoing like an orchestra. The sound of my mother's infectious laughter is pure joy and can rival your favorite thing. - Her presence is omni present.

Sometimes like an imposing shadow a reminder that she is always here with me by my side. Sometimes Mommy's memory is like a song that you cannot stop humming–full of melody, hope and love of family. It is as bright and present as a hovering star, the brightest star on any night and elicits the pleasurable sound of awe. But no thing, nor time, could hush that sweet sound of her laughter in my memory.

As a child, I always thought the worst thing that could happen to someone was the loss of one's mother. At that time, I was also sorry for my school friends who were not catholic. I thought when they died, they were going to hell.

At my Mom's funeral I noticed the headstone which was disturbed with my daddy's name on it. My mom was going to rest in his embrace. I cried out for Daddy, who had been dead for almost 30 years, by then. My bewildered adult son held me, lost, questioning. "Why are you crying out for Daddy?" I blabbered and slobbered about to fall on my face. Then my son saw my father's disturbed headstone also, while everyone was crying for Mommy. My son and I began to mourn and weep for my daddy. (I had given my eldest sister the last $30.00 needed to get that headstone erected) Meanwhile at the cemetery in N. J. my brilliant two-year-old granddaughter was looking up and around and she said, " I have so much family."

My beautiful mother trusted me. She always made me feel that whatever choices I made were wise. My mother told me I never worried about you except when you were pregnant as a teenager. We laughed, talked, and danced a lot. My husband used to tease me about how I sat at my mother's feet whenever she visited our home. He would joke about it "Why don't you just sit in her lap? You know that's what you want to do!"

We lost my brother five months after my Mom. I often recall how grounded and rooted I was. I reflect inwardly and see the fruit of my father's words 'You walk with alacrity. Like you have somewhere to go and something to do." I took my dad's cue. That little girl has purpose and is always on purpose to reach her destiny. Often when I see a picture of my mom, I blow her a kiss and I ask where is my daddy?

This haunts me and my heart still bleeds for refugees and immigrants. When my piece on immigration was published, the editor had a few questions. 1) She thought I wanted to tell my whole life's story. She did not understand the relevancy of Malcolm X's assassination. I added that piece because his mother was an immigrant 2) She wanted more information about the chores I did.—My employer was pleased with my work. But she must have been looking for justification as to why I was not paid in full as agreed upon.

———

At a Writer's Retreat, I was asked to be a Human Library at the first session and most of the people I interacted with at the event thought I might have been caught up in a trafficking game making me dependent on them with wild promises and familiarity- yet the immigrants and refugees are maligned.

At the end of the third week, I ran - I was allowed to go to my family's home on a Friday night and returned on Sunday- after the third week- I never returned to their home - and they never called to see what happened to me - was I ill? Most likely they thought they had me in the palm of their hand because I needed that green card to stay in America - But God my heavenly Father had showered me with His Divine favor. I already had the green card in my possession - with the swift wave of God's hand my green card was not mailed to the employer for security as was the norm but my family's home- two days before I arrived in NYC. My cousins stayed at their sponsors in their line of duty as "foreign maids" for at least a year before they were given their green cards - they left the employment shortly thereafter -

Elizabeth P Brooks

Corrupted Riches

You have condemned and killed the just
Walking with your own lust
you strut in your cloak of maliciousness
You are blinded because you refuse to see
In your heart or soul - you reject any and everything
That conflicts with your existing beliefs.

Sometimes indirect subtle but always intentional
You stitch a biased thread of social injustice woven in
sections and textures a delicate and
seductive dance underlying that
which belie my naivete and innocence

But my battle belongs to my Lord, the Lord you
clearly don't know

You sidestep in your hustle and flow, arrogance half –
truths one of your opiates.

Incongruent with truth and lies
Unaware of harmony and humility
When will the healing begin?

Jesus is watching I believe there is a difference with
wisdom and foresight
obedience deception and lies.

You don't hear our pain and our cries but ultimately
that will be your demise

You represent humanity's dark side.

To you, slavery was also legal, but to me it was
wicked and vile; and willful celebrations were upheld
by despicable slave masters.

To instill fear, several heads of
 slaves and charred bodies **
were displayed on the sides of the road—
while some white families and friends
including your children celebrated the event
as if it were harvest time…

Red blood dripping from black bodies;
bodies which were traumatized;
like it were grapes from your new wine press;
Quite an accomplishment.

I am deeply sorry so much quantity of evil was
allowed to seep into your spirit and your soul
your DNA, down to your descendants[12].

---

12 **Inspired by Strange Fruit by Billie Holliday
© 2020 Elizabeth P. Brooks

Unashamed

They hiss and wag their heads
Unknowingly
But clearly visible
Through opaline glass panels
Not luminous
Incapable
Of producing light
Which keeps my community
Under siege
Oh! This has gone on far too long
Too far and beyond
And when one is in grave pain
There is no one to turn to
Nowhere to go
To get justice
When the world is broken
And against you.

You cry, you vex your spirit
You bawl, then you empty
Your bosom, your belly, yourself
You empty yourself
Completely to the Lord
You turn to Jesus
With outstretched arms
He says forgive.

Continuously forgive.

13

Nominated for Best of the Net Anthology 2017

Prelude to "Needles and Pins" Poem

I was asleep and about to move into a state of wakefulness, conscious though not awake. At that time the following poem "Needles and Pins" erupted from my soul throughout my body, tossed and wrestled me around, left me sore and bruised in a stupor, speechless.

I could not talk to anyone for two whole days. I did not know what to tell them. I could not explain what had occurred. The poem erupted out of me and wrote itself. There was no explanation. It was experiential. I had no idea when I wrote it down. I was still stunned. The third day was Election Day 2016 and my phone died. The day after election I went to my provider and bought a new phone. I had not spoken to anyone for four days since that occurrence with the poem "Needles and Pins." The image of that woman in the poem is indelible in my mind. I will recognize her when I see her picture. Several weeks and months had passed, and I did not look for her though her image was haunting. I kept seeing her in the ripples of my mind. She is carved into the walnut design.

Yet at the traffic light, I stopped at red and I bowed my head when, out of nowhere, a banner, a whisper of knowing slipped across my brain. I got the name, Mary McLeod Bethune. I cried and cried in shock but still doubted because I know what she looks like. I accepted the knowing, the whisper of the Holy Spirit.

Months later, I was compelled to look for the face in my poem. Faces of black women who changed our world and "I saw her pleasant face her grace." It was the face of young Ms. Mary McLeod Bethune. My colleagues encouraged me to send the poem to the Bethune-Cookman University.

Elizabeth P Brooks

Needles and Pins

Needles & Pins
Pins & Needles
not in my hands, feet
or body but in my spirit
I open my eyes, I am wound up
like a tortured soul.
Which one of us will be
Stopped or shot next?

I am afraid to witness
another lynching
Oh, something is coming,
coming through my Spirit
I begin to hum an
unknown Negro spiritual
and I wave my arms and walk
throughout my home
and I hum and I moan from deep within.

Then I see a proud black woman
from back in the day and the
Holy Spirit carries her
with a quiet dignity
and I heard His whisper, you will
not be stripped of your humanity,
and she treads on needles & pins.

I witness her pleasant face, her grace
I dry my bitter tears from streaming
down my face - our souls are
tied together. Though she can't
see me, I am she and she is me.

We reflect then and now
still living in fear. OH! How do we reconcile?

How do we save our kind our skin our kin?
Jesus, You have shown righteous
anger, with the money changers.
I am laying this trouble
this burden of my people at the foot of
Your cross.

This battle is wickedness and pure evil.
But because of Your Divinity.
Like that woman, I too can be carried
with a quiet dignity and maintain
my humanity
Holy Spirit, You are my witness
As I tread, on needles & pins.

Pins & needles, Jesus, I know you will
Fix this! Because only You can calm my soul
Only You are - the Light of the World.

Elizabeth P Brooks

I Speak to the Shame

To give voice to my heart and my spirit
I must speak to the shame
the legality of rogue bounty hunters,
in black, khaki, and blue
licensed with badges, insignias too
Signifying rank and membership
in gangs of unjust laws social Injustice
demanding order, immoral behavior.

How many poems do I have to write
About those they dehumanize?
How many times do we have to cry?
How many dead do we have to count?
How many more names do we have to remember?

I speak to the shame of those who remain silent,
do not condemn but give implicit consent
by excusing and not accusing!

I speak to the shame of the necessity
to coin a phrase Black Lives Matter

I speak to the shame of human sacrifice
that is legalized 15-year-old child,
Jordan Edwards, innocent non-threatening but
threatened and killed the rationale –
he fit the profile of a fugitive, a black child.

I speak to the shame of the pretenses
of investigations. I speak to the shame
of police action always deemed reasonable
Shot point blank range, between the chest
through the head, behind the back riddled,
even choked....to death

160

I speak to the shame of massive
deception and public fraud –
justification of government employed protectors –
SOME who manifest as predators

I speak to the shame I speak to the shame
of those without a conscience. I speak
to the shame of the arrogance of supremacy

I speak to the shame of hypocrisy
In our country and lack of humanity,

I speak to the blatant disdain. With my words,
my heart and my spirit

I speak to the shame, I speak to the less,
the ness the shamelessness ,
the mess of shame. Shame, Shame, Shame.
Inspired by l Corinthians 6:5

I speak to your shame. Is it so, that there is not a wise
man among you
no, not one that shall be able to judge between his
brethren? (KJV)

Elizabeth P Brooks

I Want You Gone

You have no vision and are afraid
to see the grimace on my face
ashamed to see the scorn in my eyes,
embarrassed by your broken promise.

Can you hear the uproar, the horror, feel the pain?
Should I consider you an unwilling victim?
a woman conned?

It would soothe my spirit - were I to see a tear-
stained face, tormented with swollen lips,
like mine, by what you continue to uphold.

Yet, you stand there beguiling and demure,
without mercy, compassion or empathy
for humanity. In the midst of our lifetime
of tension and conflict, you persist
as a treacherous and deceptive symbol.

I wish you cared enough to take a stand
instead of just standing there.
But you are just an empty stone,
shallow, no heart, demonic, just a farce.

Your secret codes reveal yet
another contradiction, ball and chain
as your sword represents the swiftness
in which it yields injustice.
Your scale is a sham, lady.

Lady Justice - I want you gone!

When you look at people of color with disdain and see hate
and wretchedness, it is a reflection of you.

Soul Sister, Soul Sister

You are light beauty and strength
your beautiful copper color is pure unique natural
and exotic. Gurrll you rock! With you there is no surprise
you make maximum impact an obvious target attacked by
your environment
used by man in a variety of ways
yet, wide eyed you embrace all that you see
the poor the oppressed
the refugee from far and wide
lifting your fist so high
displaying hope
a welcoming beacon in the sky
with certainty, all can see
for what you stand
with clarity
your halo, your crown
reflecting the brilliant light of the
sun above and without a doubt
what you stand on
with integrity and tenacity
you trample on the hidden though visible ugly chains of
injustice
all darkness of slavery. Oh Freedom
my soul sister my Statue of Liberty!

Elizabeth P Brooks

Sunrise and Sunsets

God reveals Himself to us in many ways throughout our days, which are showered with gifts and blessings.

Everyday amassed with pomp and grandeur He displays the depth of our hope in the rays of color and prism spectrum. As I look out my window, I am swallowed up by dawn's first yawn. I inhale and exhale God's promise with gratitude. It is promised in the blessings of a sunrise.

I hear voices, the intricate bass, the stillness and mystery of the ocean and rivers and springs. God is all inclusive. He dots the land with ponds, and lakes which generate and sustain life.

Electric rainstorms create the splendor and grandeur of rainbows. The gratitude of sunsets is repeated without duplication as it bids us adieu.

Our senses give us time to receive the message. We already know who the messenger is.

Indescribable Pleasure

There is an indescribable
burning, yearning
inside of me
knowing there is
something more
beyond
unopened doors,
yet for me to unfold
and to discover.
I'm always startled
by the abundance
of beauty
that surrounds me
the majestic
sprawling canopies
of forever green
and bearded oak trees
The daily
kiss and flow
of the gliding sparkling
scenic Hillsborough river
leaves me gasping for breath
it is sometimes sprinkled
with a blanket of fresh
fallen young leaves
reflecting God's
constant goodness
and His presence
His abounding power
and mercy
I'm reminded
of the ocean and its roar
ebb and splash
billowing waves
white foam

suggesting an appetite
a sensation
undulating in a cadence
and rhythm
so beguiling and captivating
it beckons me
shouts, says my name
stirs the fire in my soul
with an immersing
and trembling pleasure
It ultimately consumes me
absorbs me
I am complete
in its presence
it complements my beauty
and the mystery within me
if I am still, long enough
I lose myself
all of my senses
and we become one
I wish the sun
would melt me, smelt me
into the sugar-powdered sand
when the tides rise
and the surf breaks
it would engulf me
take me
pull me into
a sweet forever dance
with the sea
splashing me, thrusting me
back forth
loving me to freedom.[14]

Look At Me

When I awake at the break of day
and I listen to the highlights of overnight
I'm quickly reminded of how much you struggle
with my blackness
another brutal incident,
an indictment of ugliness
grief, pain, sin, and shame
and I endure your criticisms,
your attitude your low expectations,
but you too, are a victim of the establishment
yet you very subtly oppress me
with built in systems that sanitize and legalize
the perpetrations. I am constantly sideswiped
and you are oblivious.

Bewildered, I look at my reflection in the mirror
and I see what God my heavenly Father sees in me.

So, I boldly accentuate my looks, full lips,
my natural hair, braids,
dreadlocks or nappy
for variety, fun and flavor
I can add extensions and or color and that
does not define me, deep down,
I'm very clear about my character.

But I'm forced though blessed to turn to my hub,
my spiritual mentors in my community.

We have to consciously strategize
how to promote ourselves,
how to protect ourselves, our children - who we are.
But you and I must engage in dialogue that's
enlightening and nurturing to both sides.

Elizabeth P Brooks

You cannot continue to walk around uninformed and
with blinders on. You see, there is value in diversity
but
it takes knowledge and sensitivity but what's
lacking here clearly is empathy. Look!
look at me, look at minorities collectively
to some we maybe a succulent thing,
to others sweet and sour to more still, a bit too tart.

But it takes insight to look deep within
below the surface of the melanin
of my beautiful skin.

It's not just cafe-latte, espresso, cocoa-tea,
cinnamon, molasses, dates or brown sugar.
But you are unable to recognize that this is where
my faithful spirit, and my humanity is housed
and flows throughout. I'm confident because it washes
and it cleanses me
that's why I am the epitome of beauty.

I stand on faith to duplicate
With knowledge and certainty
my vision, my mission, my wisdom,
my outward look,
my inner beauty
which is radiant with His Abundant Joy
and that - is my victory.

My constant joy, my gratitude, my dignity
and yes, my humility, these are
the attributes that enhance my beauty.

I know who I am,
I know whose I am
I am more than they think I am.
Look at Me!

Inspired by Dr. Martin Luther King Jr. I had the honor and privilege to spend two nights with my son, one of my granddaughters, and a cousin at The Retreat House, in Historic Penn Center. This is where Dr. King began to write his "I Have a Dream" speech.

Elizabeth P Brooks

Full Circle

Father God, nothing is hidden from You!

You know my brokenness,
my foolishness my pain.
Still, You have blessed me with beautiful gifts.
I was a child caught up in a whirlwind,
ventured into the unknown,
outmatched, outwitted, outsmarted.

Now, adorned with ex- husbands and enough
lovers, I have tossed aside
to recognize, the archer was an impostor.
With a deceitful bow, he couldn't
shoot an arrow.

I know now that wasn't Cupid - then -
it had to be, Marvin Gaye's music in me
in my head, groovin' to "Sexual Healing."
And David Rudder's Soca "praising me
as a bacchanal lady. Marvin and David
you promised carnal pleasure,
but it was all unquenched fire,
what's left is the remnant of a bitter root
embedded within. Unaware of the truth,
in search of intimacy, I felt my passion
build then wane again, unfulfilled.

Dissatisfied, disillusioned!
For me real love was elusive,
but I have a joyous spirit and a joyful heart
It is my ground of being, it's where I come from;
a place which glows and blooms;
where an eagle can renew its wings,
so, I pressed on; hungering for something

170

different, and there He was.

He waited! He knew I would come.
I'm rescued, redeemed not condemned.
Drenched in true love, now my thirst is
finally quenched by my master, the fountain
of the living waters. I'm the woman at the well.

I am overwhelmed.
I always wanted to be the way He designed me.
Thank you Lord! Oh Jesus!
My Lord and my King, I am now free.
Come and See!

Many years ago one of my boyfriends started to tell me a story about an old girlfriend and he said her name is Pascalle . Immediately I said, "I love that name." I had never heard it before and without missing a beat I said I was going to change my name to Pascalle. I changed it shortly after during the process of obtaining my American Citizenship. No jealousy here, I knew it was an Anansi story. But the name attracted me deep within my spirit. He said I dub you Pascalle. God's timing is perfectly planned. He has always been orchestrating my life. This was the only man in my life with whom I attended church every Sunday. It was not a Christian church, but a new age thing. Coincidently, long after my boyfriend passed away, I discovered that Pascalle means "relating to Easter." "The resurrection," "open door". The name originates from the Latin word Pascha, which came from the Hebrew word Pesach, "Passover" it is referred to as the "Easter candle" or the "Christ candle". I absolutely love my name much more after that discovery. God continues to give me revelation. It appeared to be a simple name change more than 25 years ago. A name with meaning and intention, very powerful and directs me to the Light. What a precious gift. By the grace of God, I walked into another open door. God sees our needs and He never gave up on me. He is a light unto my path.

Elizabeth P Brooks

Somehow[15]

It was not war
that allowed me
to discover
that life is filled
with enormous blessings
and opportunities
It was not a riot
that inspired me
to search beyond
my fears
and inadequacies
It was not rage
that fanned the burning
flame inside of me
to insist on love and
absolute beauty
Somehow
it was -You
You became
the source of
my power
it was You
who ignited my hunger.[16]

This piece was written in an effort to find solace after the
LA Riots. I was in college at the time. There was no way
to bury my pain and anguish. I saw no activity on campus,
and I needed an outlet. I went from class to class in a silent
tunnel. It seemed like it was just another day but my world
had changed however, during my last class of the day, the

15 **Somehow** along with **You May Applaud Now** made the finalist list for
Pushcart Prize in the same year (2017).
16 © *1992*

homework assignment was to write a poem about "self-discovery." How brilliant! I buried a lot of anguish and pain after writing the above poem. When I returned to class the following week, I was too shy to read my poem. I just turned it in. My professor was very thrilled with it. She reminded me that I should write every day.

Elizabeth P Brooks

Crystal Tear

Have you ever been in bed wide awake - in awe over
someone - or worry with wonder until daybreak?

Have you ever had a tear that welled up in your eye
and spilled over the reservoir?

Have you ever heard the tinkle, the chip, the pop of
the crystal in your tear as it dropped?

Have you ever felt the fountain of tears in your
valleys, mountains and rocks
As it trickled down your neck to your chest when you
released the waterfall onto your burdened breast?

That's a reminder that you are God's perfect treasure
when you cry it is a cleansing – evidence of a healing
and the presence of the Holy Spirit
the comforter allows the living water to flow like a
crystal river

Have you ever cried over the glory of the Lord as
He demonstrates His power and showers you with
blessings?

Have you cried over the beauty and the love and the
mystery of Jesus?

Oh, that's when your hear the tinkle of the crystal in
your teardrops
and angels singing praises to our Lord in a chorus.

Your Reflection

You love to talk to me
in the mirror
when I'm putting on my
make-up
a brilliant piece
would come to me
a thought or phrase
and I would smile
and catch a glimpse
of You.

Your Presence captured
in the reflection of
my eyes
and a broad smile
You appear in
an instant
a joyous twinkle
a brief subtle
but momentous
reflection that I
wish to recreate.

But I have to
wait and
until someday in the mirror
we will meet again
so personal and sweet.

It validates who I am
deeply fulfilled and complete.

Elizabeth P Brooks

Scriptures Empowered Me

Scriptures empowered me and they told me to take steps day by day; as I embraced the presence of God and cried out for my healing, physical, emotional and spiritual.

I meditate all day long. I have immersed myself in the word of God. I have found a lot of information and revelation by studying The Bible, a well spring. I find the Holy Bible to be prophetic, romantic, poetic and revealing. I am showered in God's grace and experience divine favor and I praise HIM all day long. For small things, large and the unexpected and anticipated things. It has been a joy discovering some of God's promises. But His timing is everything.

"Thy word is a lamp unto my feet and a light unto my path" Psalm 119:105
Everywhere I step is blessed.
God has turned my mourning into dancing Psalm 30:11 and He has given me beauty for ashes.

"The people of the land have used oppression, and exercised robbery, and have vexed the poor and needy; they have oppressed the stranger wrongly." Ezekiel 22:29 (KJV)

My fervent prayer daily:
I begin my day with the Christian Armor of God Ephesians 6:12-18. I have discovered that the devil does not rest he will come to steal our joy, but I won't give my joy away. I fight daily for my health, my faith, my family and my friends and my church. I pray for everyone. We are all God's children. "Pleasant words are a honeycomb sweet to the soul and health to the bones." Prov. 16:24 (KJV) "Trust in the Lord with all your heart and lean not unto your own understanding; in all your ways acknowledge Him and he shall direct your paths. Do not be wise unto your own eyes, fear the Lord and depart from evil, it will be health to your flesh and strength to your bones."
176

Prov 3:5-8 (NKJV).

Holy Father, please quench my flesh and magnify my spirit for Your honor and glory, in the name of Jesus Your blessed son my LORD and my King. I want every gift and plan you have for me. I now see myself the way God sees me or at least I decree that every morning. Every morning when I arise, I will speak and expect divine favor to surround me. No obstacles can stop me, and no hindrances can delay me. My battle belongs to the Lord, and it has already been won. God is exalted, the devil is defeated, and I am a child of victory.

I have discovered all that God wants is my obedience; to become intimate with HIM. I declare with authority, "Today, Elizabeth has gained wisdom and stature and Divine Favor with God and man." Luke 2:52

"Jesus has given us authority to trample over serpents and scorpions, and over all the power of the enemy, and nothing will harm us." Luke 10:19. Whenever fear, anxiety, bodily discomfort and pain seep into my soul, the only solution is to replace these thoughts and renew my mind with scripture. Prayers as simple as the Lord's Prayer, Psalm 23 or Psalm 91 which are prayers of protection. I praise God always. I practice my greatness and declare "Greater is He who is in me than he who is in the world." There are so many promises of God with which I am unfamiliar. I'm just a babe in the woods. Yet I can count my blessings that HE showers upon me with abundance, Thank You Jesus!

Today I am no longer a patient at a certain doctor's office. Thank you Jesus!

This is just part of the work and the attention I have explored spiritually that brings me to this place of discovering the Holy Spirit and my Lord and savior. Alleluia!

There are still moments when I am mentally and physically challenged. But it has been a beautiful blessing and a remarkable journey. A few months ago, I performed poetry at a formal event at church. Pastor Dwane and Lady Indera were more hopeful than I was. I had no idea what I would be able to express, but I trusted God. Though I am not a speaker on any topic, my poetry is compelled to flow out. I would sing of the goodness of God.

Take a Knee

Like Colin Kaepernick
Or take a knee like a cop
The heartless drum
of a cop on the beat
His hand in his pocket
for added pressure and swagger
to take a life for possibly
a counterfeit 20 dollars
But George Floyd was
breaking the law how many
counterfeit laws have you broken?

A cry for help on bended knee
Always a plea, obvious supplication,
painfully a humble petition,
to you it's a disgrace to the flag
you don't stop to think
let's re-consider- the flag
though symbolic it still is a thing
being blinded like lady justice
you don't consider for one moment
your logic to be flawed,
idol worshiping but wasn't this
country founded on Christianity?
Jesus was a warrior. He fought
for the poor and the oppressed
He taught us to LOVE people
and USE things
At least you operate with
Some consistency
Veterans go to war
On behalf of the flag,
and dedicate their lives
some who are not dead return

crippled physically mentally
and emotionally .

Veterans make up 6% of the population
8 % of that is the homeless population
according to the Military Times.
They sleep on sidewalks on the ground
That's not considered desecration
Does not stir your soul
disturb your heart, knowing full well
a person can be fined or be imprisoned
if they desecrate the flag, by having it touch or
being trampled on the ground
there is an imbalance here
a lack of integrity I urge you to consider
what evokes your humanity
what would Jesus do
or what is common decency
how do you define good or bad
simple morality, respect, and human dignity?

Cry Out

Freedom is significant, always heralded,
Celebrated, anticipated, pregnant
with possibilities. It is a birth from
chaos, a collective gasp.

Then the voices and the senses
cry out again for peace
cry out again for equality
cry out for justice
cry out to dismantle the corruption of
the madness of the new system.

Free consumers find themselves
living on the edge with limited privilege.

They sacrifice and spend hard earned dollars
for unsavory choices, while being preyed upon.

They ingest but are unable to digest
the deceptive business practices
and toxic ingredients from big businesses,
particularly in food and pharmaceutics.

Insulting humanity.

Many practices of corruption become the
accepted standard, the norm.

The goal and the dream of big businesses
is not about morality, not about equality, not about
harmony nor stability. The irony is, big business'
model for freedom is buying politicians, consequently
disregarding the quality of life, eroding human
dignity.

That is the outcome.
The engine is propelled by greed and dishonesty.
Cry out!

It is my right to be seen, and heard, and march, and kneel, and vote, and speak respectfully.

It is my right to show my pain, my righteous anger.

If you listen we will all learn how to live with human dignity.

I have learned in my growth that responsibility is not about my burden, your shame guilt or blame but the willingness to see myself /ourselves as cause in a matter. It is very liberating. I constantly ask what can I do to achieve better results? What can I do to demonstrate my integrity and express passion for humanity? It is so satisfying.

I choose to embrace foregiveness, trust, peace, love and joy. My passion and empathy for humanity comes from Divine Inspriation. I let it flow!

Meshed with Flesh

Good God Almighty
I speak and give voice to the blood
that is spilled, fluid platelets
proteins and other elements
in dirt, on rock, sand, and stone
lives sacrificed – flesh meshed
oxygen drained
from our very existence
Yet we enriched this land.

This land red-lines me from reaping.

Yet the sweat,
the seeds sown by my people
enriched you yesterday
and continue today.

But one day, for you
there will be no tomorrow
because of the good God I serve
and the God I know,
the good God I pray to.

The violent wind howls
and blows designed to fill us
with emptiness, soulful cries,
and brokenness. Brokenness
of women, mothers, fathers and
children. Some aware of your acrimony are
fearful for my people.

Misanthropy is inherent in your nature
but to you it's just another massacre.

Elizabeth P Brooks

Oppressing the poor in order to enrich oneself,
and giving to the rich, will lead only to loss.

- Proverbs 22:16

Long Stem Glasses

Long stem glasses
sexy and appealing
I fell into the trap of
glamorizing.
At night I enjoyed
my long stem glass
with robust red wine
had a drink or two
now that the object
has been defined
I broke the hook
that got me.

No, not my long stem glass
it's the drink
that almost got me
believing I needed one
every night
but my glass can still
seduce me.

Now I enjoy water, juice or
unsweetened tea in my goblet,
alcohol I choose
not to have it
not any day, night or
celebration.
My mind feels free
my body much
better and healthier
talked to a few of my peeps
who agreed with me
their minds and their
bodies too are now free.

Elizabeth P Brooks

You May Applaud Now![17]

We are BEAUTIFUL
We are pumps, lace, silk and satin
long skirts, boots, short skirts, sequins, pearls
leather, leggings, and jeggings
We are educators, doctors, writers, and lawyers
 power suits, power dress, diamonds,
 Bangles and rings.
We are astronauts, actors, artists, students and
athletes,
nurses and caregivers.

We are Nobel prize winners in every category,
 in literature and peace, chemistry, and physics
medicine and economics
because we are believers, givers, fighters, and
protectors.

We are mothers, friends, lovers, pastors, politicians,
vice presidents and wives
we are royalty, CEO's, and CFO's
Yes, we are in the boardroom and a force to be
reckoned with.

We are resilient, perceptive, and wise,
 your sixth sense, your conscience your universe.

We are the lighter side of you,
 we are the depths you want to conquer
we are gentle, passionate, kind, beguiling, saucy and
sassy we are Mother Earth and Mother Nature
naturally, we give birth.

---

17 **You May Applaud Now** along with **Somehow** made the finalist list for
Pushcart Prize in the same year (2017

We are the progenitor of ideas at times we are not
what you see
but we are what you get.

A lot of trappings sometimes too much baggage
or overstuffed carry-on luggage.

We can be your worst nightmare —historically, a
hurricane or your most vivid delightful dream
which takes you through the bliss of death and dying
reverberating – weeping, spent and we bring you
back again-
but full of joy and sometimes laughter
you are given a second wind you can breathe again –
to dream again.

Oh! We are very worthy of your praise
and we are everywhere,
but you are a part of us and we, you.

We are BEAUTIFUL!
and we will not be abused nor be denied
you are no better than us nor we any less than you
yet by His Grace, we birthed you
you are the gift,
now it is time for us to nurture you
and we are well-quipped
because we are bold, fearless, and God-Inspired
women of GFC - Ybor City

We are Beautiful!

I'll take my bow!

I will not be silent or silenced

Praise God!